STUDY GUIDE
PERRY M. ROGERS

THE HERITAGE OF WORLD
CIVILIZATIONS

VOLUME ONE: TO 1650

FOURTH EDITION

CRAIG · GRAHAM · KAGAN · OZMENT · TURNER

PRENTICE HALL, *Upper Saddle River, NJ 07458*

ISBN 0-13-263716-2
Printed in the United States of America

Introduction

This edition of the *Study Guide/Workbook* is designed to help students derive a greater understanding of the history presented in the third edition of Craig, Graham, Kagan, Ozment, and Turner, *The Heritage of World Civilizations*. The *Study Guide* has therefore adopted the organizational format of the textbook and focuses the main themes and historical issues that are presented in the text. The use of this *Guide* will help students test themselves in a variety of ways on their understanding of the historical material. Instructors may want to assign specific sections of the *Study Guide* as homework to be submitted for evaluation in order to monitor class comprehension of specific material on broad historical themes, primary sources, and maps. Each chapter is divided into the following sections:

COMMENTARY:

This section provides an abbreviated historical narrative of the main events, personalities, and historical themes presented in the chapter. It is not designed to supplant the textbook, but rather help students focus on the most important details that are essential in establishing a firm understanding of the history.

KEY POINTS AND VITAL CONCEPTS:

Sometimes students feel overwhelmed with the amount of material that they are expected to master in a college history class. This section provides a short analysis of the most important concepts included in the chapter and elaborates with additional information often of a comparative nature that affords perspective and promotes thoughtful analysis of issues and ideas. This section often includes chronologies that will help students orient themselves to the flow of history. Definitions of important concepts, geopolitical perspective, and specific historical problems form the subject matter of this rubric.

IDENTIFICATION TERMS:

This section includes a list of the most important people, places, institutions, ideas, and literature contained in the chapter. It does not pretend to be comprehensive, but seeks to provide a diverse selection. Students may write their identification definitions in the spaces provided and hand it into the professor as homework, or they may elect to use it as a study tool. The section requests that students explain who or what the identification term is, about when did it happen, and most importantly <u>why</u> the term is significant within the wider context of history. Note that the definition and chronological orientation are regurgitative in nature, but the "why" section is analytical and calls for a judgment on the part of the student. This part should be emphasized and is in keeping with the analytical nature of the history itself. Page references have been included so that students may locate the term quickly in the textbook.

MULTIPLE CHOICE:

Multiple Choice questions are often used to monitor a basic understanding of the chapter's historical details. This section provides fifteen questions which attend to this need, but also include questions that test a student's knowledge of concepts, chronology, and terms. These challenging questions are not composed in order to "trick" a student or to provide leading and obfuscating information, but seek a rather sophisticated, comprehensive understanding of the chapter's historical detail and general conclusions. The presentation of the question is closely tied to the narrative account in the textbook; students will find it easy to locate the questions within the text especially since the answers provided in the Answer Key section at the end of the chapter are linked to specific pages in the textbook.

STUDY QUESTIONS:

Each chapter includes six analytical Study Questions that are tied to the main historical themes presented in the textbook. They probe deeper historical questions and therefore require answers that are more comprehensive than those demanded from a Multiple Choice question. Students will not necessarily find the complete answers to these questions in the textbook because they call for conclusions that are ultimately subjective in nature. This section emphasizes comparative analysis of cultures, religious questions, political ideas, economic interpretations, and geopolitical problems. Students may therefore review and test their knowledge of the broader historical themes that will often form the basis for essay questions on exams.

DOCUMENT QUESTIONS:

The study of primary sources is one of the best ways of eliminating the veil of history and communicating directly with the ideas and values of past civilizations. Each chapter includes four Document Questions that are directly linked to the historical documents, photographs, and literature which is excerpted in the textbook. The questions seek specific interpretive analysis and emphasize perspective. Some ask for comparisons to be made with other sources in different chapters; this establishes an appreciation for the continuity of history.

MAP ANALYSIS AND MAP EXERCISE:

This section asks the student to view and analyze particular maps in the textbook. The Map Analysis section presents the geopolitical boundaries of a region and seeks to engage the student visually in determining causation through logic and with reference to geography. The Map Exercise provides the student with a geographical foundation by asking the student to locate specific places, civilizations, rivers, mountains, bodies of water, etc. on a map provided in the *Study Guide* itself. By doing this exercise, the student will be familiar with the basic geography of the region which in turn will provide common reference points that should aid and focus class discussions.

CONTENTS

INTRODUCTION iii

CHAPTER 1 - *Birth of Civilization* 1

CHAPTER 2 - *The Four Great Revolutions in Thought and Religion* 15

CHAPTER 3 - *Greek and Hellenistic Civilization* 29

CHAPTER 4 - *Iran, India, and Inner Asia to 200 C.E.* 45

CHAPTER 5 - *Republican and Imperial Rome* 59

CHAPTER 6 - *Africa: Early History to 1000 C.E.* 75

CHAPTER 7 - *China's First Empire (221 B.C.E.- 220 C.E.)* 89

CHAPTER 8 - *Imperial China (589-1368)* 101

CHAPTER 9 - *Japan: Early History to 1467* 115

CHAPTER 10 - *Iran and India Before Islam* 129

CHAPTER 11 - *The Formation of Islamic Civilization (622-945)* 141

CHAPTER 12 - *The Early Middle Ages in the West to 1000:*
The Birth of Europe..155

CHAPTER 13 - *The High Middle Ages (1000-1300)* 167

CHAPTER 14 - *The Islamic Heartlands and India (CA. 1000-1500)*............................183

CHAPTER 15 - *Ancient Civilizations of the Americas* 197

CHAPTER 16 - *The Late Middle Ages and the Renaissance in the West*
(1300-1527)...211

CHAPTER 17 - *The Age of Reformation and Religious Wars* 225

CHAPTER 18 - *Africa (CA. 1000-1800)* 241

CHAPTER 19 - *Conquest and Exploitation: The Development of the*
Transatlantic Economy...255

Birth of Civilization

COMMENTARY

Chapter One explores the origins of civilization in the four major river valleys of the world from prehistory to the establishment and utilization of written records. From perhaps 600,000 to 10,000 B.C.E., people were hunters, fishers and gatherers, but not producers of food. The chapter develops the social relationships within prehistoric society and contrasts them with the changes dictated by the development of agriculture - the Neolithic Revolution. By about 3000 B.C.E. writing began to develop in the Tigris and Euphrates river valleys in Mesopotamia, which was then followed in the Nile valley. Somewhat later, urban life developed in the Indus Valley of India and the Yellow River basin in China. This development did not negate the nomadic lifestyle of many groups, and the constant tension between nomadic and settled lifestyles was an important aspect of the historical development.

The Sumerian culture developed in southern Mesopotamia, near the Persian Gulf. The Sumerians contributed many important advancements in writing (cuneiform), law, education and religious thought. For example, Hammurabi's code (ca. 1750 B.C.E.) is the fullest and best preserved ancient legal code and reveals a society strictly divided by class, yet bound together by harsh precepts that demanded discipline and order. The civilization, however, was generally pessimistic in outlook, an observation based mainly on the evidence of religious sources that depict a gloomy picture of the afterworld as a "land of no return".

Egyptian civilization developed in a different manner and remained, for the most part, optimistic in its long history. Geographically, the Nile River unified the region and the desert afforded the protection from nomadic invaders necessary for the evolution of centralized political authority. Pharaonic authority was reflected in the pyramids of the Old Kingdom and the imperialism of New Kingdom dynasts, Thutmose III and Ramses II.

Indian civilization developed in a unique fashion as the early urban literate culture was superseded by the Aryan culture after a few hundred years. The chapter examines the development of the early Indian and Aryan cultures separately. The Indus or Harappan civilization developed in the region of modern Pakistan, and excavated sites dating from 2500-1500 B.C.E. show an unusual conformity in the culture based upon similar city layouts, building construction and floodwalls. Reasons for the decline of this civilization are open to speculation, but could involve abnormal flooding and/or the appearance of warlike nomads around 1800 B.C.E. The Aryan culture that "refounded" Indian civilization about 1500 B.C.E. did not develop an urban culture, but depended on stock breeding and agriculture.

Early Chinese civilization developed about 4000 B.C.E. in the Yellow River valley. The political institution was the city-state and the largest of these areas was the capital of the Shang Dynasty (1766-1050 B.C.E.). This capital moved a great deal, therefore the great monumental architecture of Mesopotamia or Egypt did not develop in China. This is an important point for comparisons between these regions. The later Bronze period developed into the Chou Dynasty (1050-771 B.C.E.), which continued the basic structure created by the Shang Dynasty. The Western Chou dynasty was overrun by barbarians in 771 B.C.E. and fled two hundred miles to the east. The Eastern Chou dynasty was never able to recover its lost authority and smaller states within the boundaries of its realm entered into defensive alliances against the power of encroaching territorial states. From 401-256 B.C.E., interstate stability disappeared as power was contested by eight or nine great territorial contenders. The rise of these territorial states at the expense of dynastic rule was due to the expansion of population and agricultural lands, the development of commerce and the rise of a new army composed of conscripted footsoldiers and professional commanders.

The chapter concludes with a section on the Prehistoric era in the Americas. Four areas of relatively dense settlement emerged in the Americas: Puget Sound (depended on fish, rather than agriculture); Mississippi valley (based on maize agriculture), Mesoamerica and the Andean region of South America. The latter two saw the emergence of strong and long-lasting states. Their remarkable skills in pottery, weaving, sculpture and architecture are most impressive. Chapter 15 examines the Mesoamerican and Andean civilization in detail.

KEY POINTS AND VITAL CONCEPTS

1. <u>Important Definitions</u>: The text emphasizes the differences between culture and civilization:
    A) <u>Culture</u>: "the ways of living built up by a group and passed on from one generation to another."
    B) <u>Civilization</u>: "a human form of culture in which many people live in urban centers, have mastered the art of smelting metals and have developed a method of writing."

2. <u>Geography and History</u>: Geographic determinism is an important factor in the unique development of all four civilizations discussed in this chapter. The agricultural advantages of the Indus and Yellow River valleys proved essential to the progress of human civilization. In the ancient Near East, geographical influence on the development of particular civilizations is even more pronounced. Egypt was protected by deserts and the sea and nourished by the Nile which flooded regularly; it was less prone to invasion and hence more secure politically. Mesopotamia was invaded regularly, having no natural barriers; the Tigris and Euphrates Rivers were difficult to navigate and control and flooded regularly. The first use of writing may have been to record the arrangements for river control. The Mesopotamian civilizations are described as more pessimistic than the Egyptian which was more secure geographically.

3. <u>The Neolithic Revolution</u>: One of the most important transitions in human history occurred in only a few Paleolithic societies. The development of agriculture and the domestication of animals for food and material and the invention of pottery dramatically changed the way people lived and worked. Reasons for the shift to the age of agriculture remain unclear, but gradually population increased and societies became more organized and stable, often resulting in urban communities and the attendant development of writing (about 3000 B.C.E. in the Near East and somewhat later in India and China). Because of the extinction of mammoths and other forms of game that had become extinct during the Ice Age, American peoples had to rely on protein from vegetable sources. One result was that their production of foodstuffs providing protein far outpaced that of European agriculture. Approximate dates for the earliest Neolithic societies follow:
    A) <u>Near East</u> (ca. 8000 B.C.E.) Based on wheat
    B) <u>China</u> (ca. 4000 B.C.E.) Based on millet and rice
    C) <u>India</u> (ca. 3600 B.C.E.) Based on wheat
    D) <u>Mesoamerica</u> (ca. 4000 B.C.E.) Based on maize

4. <u>The Birth of Civilization in World Perspective</u>: Religious development and the evolution of writing are of major importance to all early civilizations. The development of monotheism by Akhenaton in Egypt had limited impact on early evolution of religious thought. However, the Vedas and reference to divine will in both India and China were of primary importance in the evolution of their respective societies. Monumental architecture (pyramids, obelisks, temples, etc.) and the organization of empires (Egyptian, Assyrians, Shang, Aryan and others) were important factors in the evolution of world history.

IDENTIFICATION TERMS

For each of the following, tell who or what it is, about when did it happen, and why it is significant in the history of the period:

culture (p. 3):

cuneiform (p. 8):

Veda (p. 18):

Neolithic Revolution (p. 4):

Aryan (p. 19):

Brahman (p. 23):

Pharaoh (p. 11):

Bronze Age (p. 5):

Hammurabi (p. 7):

shih (p. 29):

nomes (p. 12):

Olmecs (p. 31):

Sargon (p. 7):

Harappa (p. 15):

Bharatas (p. 19):

MULTIPLE CHOICE QUESTIONS

1. Culture is best defined as
   a. the way in which many people live in urban centers, have mastered the art of smelting metals and have developed a method of writing
   b. the ways of living built up by a group and passed on from one generation to another
   c. a society where the population engages in abstract thought and promotes policies of peace rather than war
   d. the complex interrelationships among human beings which result in writing, literature and cities

2. The Code of Hammurabi was
   a. an outline of religious practice
   b. a body of civil and criminal law
   c. the moral teaching of Hammurabi
   d. a system of writing developed by the Babylonians

3. The uniformity of building construction and city layout in Harappan excavation sites suggests
   a. strong centralized government
   b. a lack of imagination and creativity in the culture
   c. the geographical isolation of the region
   d. both a and b

4. Neolithic peoples in the Americas derived their protein from
   a. mammoths and other forms of game   c. fish
   b. maize   d. both b and c

5. Because the need for record keeping was so great,
   a. public schools developed in Sumerian society
   b. a class of scribes developed
   c. the Sumerians developed an alphabetic script
   d. all of the above

6. The typical king in a river valley civilization was regarded as
   a. a god   c. the sole religious authority
   b. a delegate of a god   d. both a and b

7. The first use of writing may have been to record
   a. the deeds of kings
   b. the behavior of the river and astronomical events
   c. business transactions
   d. literature

Chapter 1

8. Sargon
    a. established a dynasty that ruled Sumer and Akkad for two centuries
    b. found ways of controlling the Tigris and Euphrates rivers
    c. conquered the "cedar forests of Lebanon"
    d. both a and c

9. Cuneiform
    a. was a writing system invented by the Sumerians
    b. developed into hieroglyphics
    c. was written on papyrus
    d. both b and c

10. The Egyptian period of greatest pharaonic authority was the
    a. Old Kingdom   c. New Kingdom
    b. Middle Kingdom   d. First Intermediate Period

11. The pharaoh Akhenaton
    a. practiced polytheism
    b. worshipped a universal deity, Aton
    c. conquered the Hittites
    d. both a and b

12. *Veda*
    a. means "text" and was the sacred book of the Aryans
    b. is a language which belongs to the Indo-European group
    c. means "knowledge" and is a collective term for Indian holy texts
    d. none of the above

13. The characteristic political institution of Bronze Age China was
    a. the agricultural state   c. a republic
    b. the city-state   d. democracy

14. The supreme "Deity Above" belonged to the
    a. Toltecs   c. Eastern Chou dynasty
    b. Vedic Aryans   d. Shang Chinese

15. Which of the following contributed to the rise of large territorial states in China?
    a. expansion of population and agricultural lands
    b. rise of commerce
    c. changes in military tactics and organization
    d. all of the above

STUDY QUESTIONS

1. What influence did the Neolithic Revolution have upon the development of world civilization? How do we know people lived before written history? Discuss the kinds of evidence we have and the reliability of this information.

2. How did the Eastern Chou civilization differ from the Western Chou? In what specific ways were the Chou civilizations different from the Shang?

3. Compare and contrast the Sumerian and Egyptian concepts of the afterlife. Develop the major aspects of their respective civilizations that brought about these developments in the ancient world. How did they differ? Why did Akhenaton try to change Egyptian religion? Why did it fail?

4. Compare the major contributions of the small nations of the Near East to world civilization before the development of the Assyrian Empire. Why is the development of iron an important factor? In what ways did the use of money alter the development of world history?

5. Why is little known about the early Indus River valley civilization in relation to other major civilizations of the ancient world? What explanations can you give for the failure of the Indus civilization?

6. How did the Neolithic period in the Americas differ from that of other early civilizations? Why has the American participation in the Neolithic Revolution been termed "remarkable"?

DOCUMENT QUESTIONS

1)   *Hammurabi Creates a Code of Law in Mesopotamia (p. 9)*:

Hammurabi's code reflected the Mesopotamian society of his time. Indicate the major features of this society as they are reflected in the code. What were the advantages and disadvantages of such a code for the structure of society?

2)   *The "Israel Stele" of the Pharaoh Merenptah (p. 13)*:

What is the subject matter of this stele? What purpose or purposes was it meant to serve? Why is it an important primary source?

3)	*Hymn to the Lord of Creatures (p. 22)*:

How does this hymn reflect the principle of sacrifice? Why is this so important? How does the creation of the four social classes provide stability in society? How could a caste society create political dissention?

4)	*Human Sacrifice in Early China (p. 27)*:

What is the meaning of this poem regarding human sacrifice? How especially do you interpret the lines, "Could we but ransom him/There are a hundred would give their lives"?

MAP ANALYSIS

Map 1-3: Indus and Vedic Aryan Cultures

Look carefully at the different Indian civilizations as noted on Map 1-3 on page 16 of the textbook. Since it is often difficult to differentiate these civilizations, it is helpful to visualize their locations on the map. Make a list of the characteristics of each civilization. Geographically, why is it likely that the Harappan Indus culture influenced the Vedic Aryan cultures?

MAP EXERCISE

Map 1-1: The Four Great River Valley Civilizations to Ca. 1000 B.C.E.

By 2000 B.C.E. civilization and urban life was established in four river valley regions. Identify these four civilizations and the rivers that helped nurture them on Map 1-1 on page 5 of your textbook and place them on the map provided on the next page of this *Study Guide*.

1. Mesopotamia and Babylonia

2. Tigris River

3. Ancient Egypt

4. Nile

5. Harappan and Vedic Civilizations

6. Ganges and Indus Rivers

7. Shang

8. Yellow River

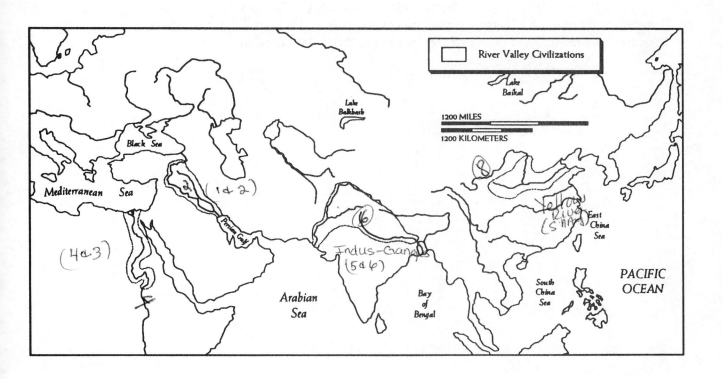

MAP 1-1
The Four Great River Valley Civilizations

MULTIPLE CHOICE ANSWER KEY *(with page references)*

1. B (3)	6. D (6)	11. B (12)
2. B (7)	7. D (5)	12. C (18)
3. A (15)	8. D (7)	13. B (24)
4. D (31)	9. A (8)	14. D (26)
5. B (5)	10. A (11)	15. D (29)

2

The Four Great Revolutions In Thought and Religion

COMMENTARY

This chapter surveys the four religious and philosophical revolutions that have shaped the subsequent history of the world and demonstrates how the societies in India, China, the Near East and Greece attempted to define humankind's relationship with the cosmos.

The four religious and philosophical movements contained many common elements. They developed in the four most advanced cultures of the ancient world. Each movement also rose from a crisis or major change in a given area such as the appearance of iron, or the outside influence of invading forces. After 300 B.C.E. there was seldom any new introduction of religious or philosophical thought and alteration to the existing systems was a process of evolution and diffusion of central concepts and ideas. Perhaps one reason for the endurance of the major cultures was the formulation of universal questions regarding the human condition. What are human beings? What is our relation to the universe? How should we relate to others?

China developed concepts around the 100 schools' ideals with Confucian, Taoist and Legalist thought being the most pronounced. A unique characteristic of Chinese thought was its view of the cosmos as a single, continuous sphere, rather than a dualism (prevalent in the West) that distinguishes between the world and a supernatural otherworld. The Chinese emperor regulated and harmonized the cosmological forces of Heaven and Earth through the power of his virtue. Therefore, intellectual divisions that occurred in other societies were not as pronounced in China.

Confucius (551-449 B.C.E.) stressed the harmony that moved from the individual family member to the state as the ideal existence and that the well-being of a society depended on the morality of its members. All ethics became a part of nature and a portion of the cosmos. Good men would then govern for the benefit of society and the common people. The king was regarded as a sage and held a preeminent position, possessing an almost mystical virtue and power. Taoism, dating from the fourth century B.C.E., offered a refuge from the social responsibilities of Confucian thought. The Tao (or Way) functioned on the cosmic level rather than on the human scale of events. The best life was to return to humankind's original simplicity or to "learn to be without learning." Two additional assumptions summarize the Taoist thought pattern: (1) that any action pushed to the extreme will create an opposite extreme; (2) that too much government, even good government, can become oppressive.

Legalism was the last great school of Chinese thought in the third century B.C.E. The Legalists were anxious to end the wars that plagued China during this time period and believed a unified country with a strong state that established laws to bring about punishment and pain would result in a properly balanced society. The laws should have incentives for loyalty and bravery in battle, for obedience, diligence, and frugality in everyday life. Human laws were thus placed above divine ethics which had been modeled in Heaven.

The Hindu faith is centered in India and developed over centuries toward a recognizable form by perhaps about 200 C.E. It is totally inaccurate to think of Hindu as a term for any single or uniform religious community. The Upanishadic sages developed the concept of existence as a ceaseless cycle, a never ending alternation between life and death; this became the basic assumption of all Indian thought and religious life. Because of the fundamental impermanence of everything in existence, the good as well as evil is temporary. The flux of existence knows only movement, change, endless cause and effect far transcending a human life span or even a world eon. To understand this process, meditation becomes the most important tenet of the belief in order to develop the inner awareness of the realities of life. This awareness can be achieved through *karma* (work or action) in that every action will have its inevitable results. Good deeds will bring good results on earth and in the afterlife.

The Jain tradition was developed by Mahavira (540-468 B.C.E.) and is an attempt to escape from the material world and its accumulations of *karma*. In the Jain view there is no end to existence, only cycles of generation and degeneration. The solution was to eliminate evil thoughts and actions, practice asceticism and the meditative discipline of yoga and thus gain enlightenment from *karma*.

Buddha (566-486 B.C.E.) established his faith on Hindu and Jain concepts, but altered them and developed a "Middle Path" between asceticism and sensual indulgence. The core of the faith is in the four noble truths: all life is suffering, the source of suffering is desire, the cessation of desire is the way to end suffering, and the path to this end is eightfold: right understanding, thought, speech, action, livelihood, effort, mindfulness and concentration. The key idea to the faith is that everything is causally linked within the universe.

The text continues with an account of Hebrew history from its origins in Mesopotamia to the destruction of the Judaic state under the Romans in 132 C.E. The *Old Testament* is the written record of the Jewish experience, and the monotheistic tenets contained therein formed the basis for Christianity and Islam and influenced the ethical and legal systems of the West. The activity of the prophets influenced the crucial events in Israelite history to the first millennium B.C.E. Two major focal points are important in the evolution of the faith. First was the significance of history in the divine plan. The second concept, or set of ideas, centered on the nature of Yahweh. God was the ideal of justice and goodness and demanded justice and goodness from his followers; thus he was a moral God. For the first time, we find a nation defined, not primarily by dynastic, linguistic or geographical considerations, but above all by shared religious faith and practice.

Greek ideas had much in common with the ideas of previous cultures, yet as early as the sixth-century B.C.E. Ionian Greeks raised questions and suggested answers about nature that produced an intellectual revolution. The attempt to understand the position of humankind in the universe and on earth created a climate of inquiry which became the foundation of Western intellectual thought. The blending of Judaic and Greek ideas brought about an expansive discussion of the relation of individuals to the cosmic order.

KEY POINTS AND VITAL CONCEPTS

1. <u>Religious Thought</u>: Hinduism, Taoism, Buddhism, Jainism and Judaism became the bases for other religious movements throughout the world. Issues such as the search for the better life, the contemplation of death and the nature of afterlife, the ceaseless cycle of existence, created an ongoing debate regarding the nature of humankind and its place in the universe. Each major religious and philosophical movement created in turn its own rebellion. Hinduism established the environment for Jainism, Buddhism and the Sikhs. Judaism was the seedbed of Christianity and eventually of Islam. Chinese reaction to Confucianism developed into the Taoist and Legalist branches which offered alternatives to Confucian ideals. All religions of the world were forced to defend their basic concepts thereby creating a more dynamic intellectual interchange in world history. The major religious and philosophical issues that divided movements have remained to the present time. Very few new concepts have challenged or resolved many of the fundamental differences of opinion.

2. <u>The Monotheistic Revolution</u>: The Hebrew state did not establish a vast empire or contribute an advanced political philosophy. In fact, the fate of this small nation would be of little interest were it not for its unique religious achievement. It developed a tradition of faith that amounted to a revolution in ways of thinking about the human condition, the meaning of life and history, and the nature of the divine. The Hebrews contributed a uniquely moralistic understanding of human life based on an uncompromising monotheism. For the first time, we find a nation defined above all by shared religious faith and practice rather than by dynastic, linguistic, or geographical considerations.

3. <u>Greek Philosophical Contributions</u>: Although Greek civilization accepted a rather amoral paganism, this was juxtaposed from the sixth century B.C.E. with a devotion to rational inquiry. The Greeks opened the discussion of most of the issues that remain major concerns in the modern world: What is the nature of the universe and can it be controlled? Are there divine powers, and if so, what is humanity's relationship with them? Are law and justice human, divine or both? What is the place in human society of freedom, obedience, and reverence? These and other problems were confronted and intensified by the Greeks.

IDENTIFICATION TERMS

For each of the following, tell who or what it is, about when did it happen, and why it is significant in the history of the period:

Anaximander (p. 62)

Analects (p. 42):

Torah (p. 58):

Cynics (p. 65):

Lao-tzu (p. 44):

Logos (p. 62):

Legalism (p. 46):

Samsara (p. 49):

Polis (p. 65):

ahimsa (p. 53):

karma (p. 50):

Sophists (p. 64):

Moksha (p. 51):

Nirvana (p. 56):

Thales (p. 61):

MULTIPLE CHOICE QUESTIONS

1. Which religious or philosophical revolution showed the greatest continuity of development over the centuries?
   a. Chinese philosophy
   b. Indian religion
   c. Judaic monotheism
   d. Greek philosophy

2. Why did the four religious or philosophical revolutions occur in areas of the original river-valley civilizations?
   a. they were relatively isolated from attack
   b. they were protected by geographical barriers
   c. these areas contained agriculture, cities, literacy, and specialized professions
   d. all of the above

3. Why did a philosophical revolution occur in China in the 3rd century B.C.E.?
   a. because of the earlier influence of Greek philosophy
   b. because of the destruction of Chinese society by the Mongols
   c. because of the disintegration of the Chou society and the rise of the merchant class
   d. because of the harsh nature of Confucianism

4. In the Chinese worldview,
   a. there is a distinct difference between this world and a supernatural world
   b. there is no distinction between this world and a supernatural world
   c. humans regulate the cosmological forces of heaven and earth
   d. both b and c

5. *The Art of War* by Sun-tzu
   a. praises the general who wins victories without battles
   b. advocates total destruction of an enemy
   c. is still relatively unknown in the West
   d. both b and c

6. In his philosophical writings, Confucius advocated
   a. social mobility and democratic government
   b. an unbroken social harmony based on an understanding of one's place and responsibility in the social order
   c. a realization that human nature was essentially bad and that it must be restrained
   d. a freedom from the burden of social responsibilities

7. Taoism offers
   a. a way of attaining power in a society dominated by social constraints
   b. a refuge from the burden of social responsibilities
   c. no political philosophy
   d. a way to use knowledge in order to create social distinctions

8. Which of the following is a basic tenet of Taoism?
   a. an action pushed to the extreme results in progress
   b. too much government, even good government, can become oppressive
   c. political democracy is the result of social responsibility
   d. true peace requires a strong political state

9. In the Upanishadic worldview,
   a. knowledge is the ultimate source of power
   b. immortality is an escape from all existence
   c. immortality is found in an afterlife
   d. both a and b

10. The best definition of *samsara* is the
    a. endless cycle of renewed existence
    b. release from existence
    c. "right order of things"
    d. realization of one's fate

11. The paramount ideal for the Jains was the concept of
    a. *ahimsa* or "non-injury"
    b. *samsara* or "transmigration of the soul"
    c. *karma* or "action"
    d. none of the above

12. Buddhism originated in
    a. India   c. Japan
    b. China   d. Nepal

13. The primary figure in the Buddhist religious tradition is
    a. Mahavira   c. Siddhartha Gautama
    b. Kshatriya   d. Dukkha

14. Which of the following is in the correct chronological order?
    a. Kind David, King Solomon, Restoration of the Temple, Destruction of Jerusalem and fall of Judah
    b. King Solomon, Destruction of Jerusalem and fall of Judah, King David, Restoration of the Temple
    c. King David, Destruction of Jerusalem and fall of Judah, King Solomon, Restoration of the Temple
    d. King David, King Solomon, Destruction of Jerusalem and fall of Judah, Restoration of the Temple

15. Which of the following Greek philosophers believed that the *polis* made individuals self-sufficient?
    a. Plato   c. Aristotle
    b. Thales   d. Anaxagoras

STUDY QUESTIONS

1. What do the four major philosophical and religious revolutions have in common in their development and impact on world history? Why are there so few religious and philosophical revolutions in history? Where did the major revolutions spread during the ancient time period?

2. What are the basic tenets of Confucian thought, how did they evolve and influence Chinese education? In what manner was Confucian thought different from other major religious and philosophical ideas? Why was there a long delay before this philosophical system became an important part of Chinese society?

3. Develop the central concept of the Tao, or the Way. Contrast this philosophical system with Confucianism and the impact on individuals in China. In what manner were there similar developments in other areas of the world?

4. Explain the two basic tenets of the Nature of Reality in the Upanishadic worldview. How was this a fundamental change from the older Vedic concepts? What is the Upanishadic belief regarding the existence of an afterlife?

5. What are the major aspects of Buddhist and Jain rebellion against Hinduism? Develop the proper historic background and time frame in your response. Why did Buddhism spread from India? In what ways are both religious movements similar and different?

6. Describe the importance of the *Old Testament* as a reliable historic source. What is the importance of a written source for a religious belief? How is the *Old Testament* different from other revealed religious texts?

DOCUMENT QUESTIONS

1)   Legalism (p. 48):

What are Han Fei-Tzu's main arguments concerning punishments? Do you regard them as simplistic or do you think the principles are workable and even eternal in application? How does Han Fei-Tzu's attack on Confucianism reflect the main ideas of Legalism?

2)   Samsara and the Monastic Virtues (p. 53):

After reading this short selection, how do you interpret the line, "He must bear it all to wear out his *karma,* and follow the noble supreme law"? What is *samsara* and how does one overcome it?

3)   *God's Purpose with Israel (p. 60)*:

   How does this selection from Jeremiah in the *Old Testament* of the *Bible* reflect God's "covenant" with the Jews? According to this source, what are the primary characteristics of Yahweh?

4)   *The Sophists: From Rational Inquiry to Skepticism (p. 64)*:

   Why are the ideas in this document considered "remarkable and even dangerous" when taken to the extreme? How is this source reflective of a "Greek spirit"? Is this type of inquiry different from the explanations sought by the other religions in this chapter?

MAP ANALYSIS

Map 2-1: Ancient Palestine

Study Map 2-1 on page 58 of the textbook. Why did the cities of Jericho, Jerusalem, Hebron, and Beersheba continue to prosper throughout the ancient world? Why was the river Jordan so important in Biblical times?

MAP EXERCISE

Map 2-1: Ancient Palestine

After the death of Solomon in the 9th century B.C.E., the kingdom of Israel split into two parts: Israel and Judah. Israel fell to the Assyrians in 722 B.C.E.; Judah to the Babylonians under Nebuchandnezzar in 586 B.C.E. Identify these places and features of ancient Palestine on Map 2-1 on page 58 of your textbook and place them on the map provided on the next page of this *Study Guide*.

1. Dead Sea	8. Jericho
2. Sea of Galilee	9. Bethlehem
3. Judah	10. Sidon
4. Israel	11. Jordan River
5. Phoenicia	12. Damascus
6. Gaza	13. Megiddo
7. Jerusalem	

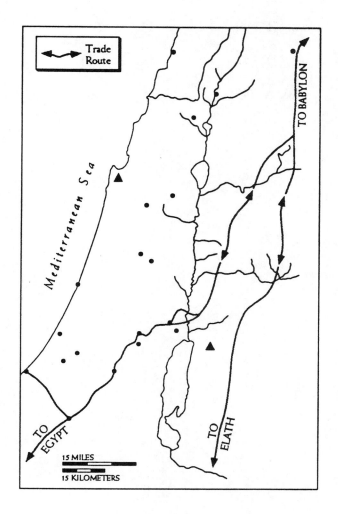

MAP 2-1
Ancient Palestine

MULTIPLE CHOICE ANSWER KEY *(with page references)*

1. A (39)	6. B (42)	11. A (53)
2. C (40)	7. B (44)	12. A (54)
3. C (41)	8. B (46)	13. C (54)
4. D (41)	9. D (49)	14. D (56)
5. A (41)	10. A (49)	15. C (68)

3

Greek and Hellenistic Civilization

COMMENTARY

The chapter begins by stressing the importance of the ancient Greeks to the history of Western Civilization. Although Greek civilization was centered in the lands surrounding the Aegean Sea, the Greeks spread their culture throughout the Mediterranean area and even into the Black Sea region, coming into contact with the older civilizations of the Near East. This chapter also surveys the political and cultural history of the Greek *poleis* in the period of their greatest power, 479-338 B.C.E., and continues the story to the eve of the Roman conquest, about 150 B.C.E.

For Greek civilization, the Bronze Age (2900-1150 B.C.E.) was centered in two regions: on the island of Crete and on the mainland of Greece itself. The people of Crete were not Greek, but had a great influence on early Greece. Our knowledge of civilization on Crete (labelled Minoan by its primary excavator Sir Arthur Evans) depends primarily on archaeological evidence obtained at Cnossus and a few other sites in central and eastern Crete. The palace complex at Cnossus is an intricate structure, labyrinthine in nature, but without defensive walls. The evidence reveals a secure, optimistic society whose gaily painted pottery was widely admired and exported.

The civilization on the mainland which flourished from ca. 1400-1200 was centered in the city of Mycenae and is called Mycenaean. The Mycenaeans, in contrast to the Minoans, were more warlike and constructed strong defensive walls. This was a wealthy society which traded with Crete and the eastern Mediterranean; the Mycenaean Greeks probably plundered Troy about 1250 B.C.E., a war which Homer immortalized in his poems.

Between 1200 and 1100 B.C.E., the Mycenaean world was shaken and destroyed by a catastrophe, traditionally attributed to an invasion by a northern people, the Dorians. Greece then entered into a period of decline called the "Greek Middle Ages" (1100-800 B.C.E.). The epic poems of Homer, although written about 750 B.C.E., depict the world of the 9th and 10th centuries, as well as of the earlier Mycenaean world.

The isolation and relative calm of the "middle ages" allowed the development of a unique Greek institution. The *polis* began to emerge between 800 and 750 B.C.E. Usually translated as "city-state", it was both more and less. Generally, it was a small independent political unit and was thought of by its citizens as a community of relatives, rather than an impersonal state. By about 750 B.C.E., the Greek *poleis* responded to population pressure by sending out colonies throughout the Mediterranean. These *poleis* retained only nominal ties with the mother, but such colonization encouraged trade and industry.

At first, Sparta was not strikingly different from other Greek *poleis*, but about 725 B.C.E., the Spartans remedied population pressure, not by colonizing, but rather by invading neighboring Messenia and enslaving its inhabitants. These slaves, who outnumbered the Spartans perhaps ten to one, were called Helots. Their existence coupled with war against Argos about 650 B.C.E., changed forever the nature of the Spartan *polis*. The Spartans chose to introduce fundamental reforms, attributed to the legendary Lycurgus, which turned their city into a military academy and camp.

The city-state of Athens developed quite differently from Sparta. In the seventh century, Athens was a typical aristocratic *polis* whose nobles served first as magistrates (*archons*) and then on the governing council (*Areopagus*). A serious agrarian crisis arose by the late 6th century and many farmers fell into debt and were enslaved by the nobility. In 594, the Athenians elected Solon as "sole archon" with extraordinary powers to remedy the problems. Solon canceled current debts and freed the debt slaves.

Solon's efforts, however were only temporarily successful. By 546, a tyrant named Pisistratus had achieved power in the state. In 510, however, with great popular support Clisthenes succeeded in overcoming his political opponents and established a democracy. This democracy eliminated many of the old regional rivalries and required that each citizen contribute his time and energy to the governance of the state, including fighting in the military and serving on juries. Clisthenes also created a new council of 500 and encouraged free and open debate in the assembly. Although his successes would give Athens an even more open and popular government, Clisthenes can be called the founder of Athenian democracy.

In the late sixth century, Greece not only faced foreign ideas, but also the threat of foreign conquest. The Persian empire had been created by Cyrus the Great in the mid-sixth century. His successors invaded Greece after Athenian aid to a rebellion in Ionia in 499 B.C.E. The Greeks repelled two invasions by the Persians in 490 and 480 B.C.E., and succeeded in defending their homeland and lifestyle; the stage was set for the achievements of Classical Greece.

After the Persian retreat from Greece, Athens emerged as the leader of a coalition of Greek states of the Aegean islands and the coast of Asia Minor (Delian League). Athens collected tribute from these states to finance a war to free those Greeks still under Persian rule, to protect all against a Persian return, and to collect booty. Cimon led the allies to victory and became the most influential statesman in Athens for nearly two decades.

Even as the Athenians were tightening control over their allies, at home they developed the freest government the world had ever seen. Under the leadership of Pericles, the powers of the aristocratic council, the *Areopagus*, were curtailed and every decision of the state had to be approved by the popular assembly. As well, jury pay was introduced and the actions of government officials were scrutinized carefully at the end of their terms. Pericles voiced the pride which the Athenians felt for their democracy in his famous Funeral Oration. The Thirty Years Peace of 445 B.C.E. lasted for only a decade. In 435, a dispute involving the island of Corcyra forced the Athenians to side against an important ally of Sparta, Corinth. The deep-seated distrust between Sparta and Athens, coupled with the aggressive arguments of Corinth resulted in a Spartan declaration of war in 432. The chapter continues with a more detailed narration of the Great Peloponnesian War which was fought, with a short period of unstable peace, for the next 27 years (431-404 B.C.E.). This long and disastrous war eventually led to the defeat of Athens and shook the foundations of Greek civilization.

In the fifth and fourth centuries B.C.E., the Greek civilization flourished and produced cultural achievements which justify the designation of Classical Period. The chapter recounts the contributions of the Attic tragedians, Aeschylus, Sophocles and Euripides, who dealt with powerful, cosmic themes and great confrontations of conflicting principles, as well as the psychology and behavior of human beings under stress. This century also produced the first prose literature in the form of history. Herodotus, the "father of history" wrote an account of the Persian Wars, while Thucydides contributed his masterpiece on the Peloponnesian War. Thucydides has been called a "scientific historian" for his devotion to accuracy and truth.

Athenian architecture and sculpture also flourished, reaching their acme in the temples of the Acropolis, above all the Parthenon. The brilliance of these buildings gave confirmation to Pericles' statement that Athens was "the school of Hellas." At the beginning of the fourth century, Macedon, the land to the north of Thessaly, was a backward, semi-barbaric kingdom, beset by civil strife, loose organization and a lack of money. In spite of these problems, Philip II rose to unify the Macedonians and lead them to victory over the Greek city-states to the south.

The chapter then proceeds to give a more detailed account of Macedonian government in Greece, the assassination of Philip and the succession of Alexander the Great. His exploits against the Persian empire are next recounted as are his death and the struggle for succession to his position and empire.

Alexander's conquest marked the end of the central role of the *polis* in Greek life and thought. Cities prospered, but without political freedom, they had only a shadow of the vitality of the true *polis*. In this new environment, most Greeks turned away from political solutions to their problems, and sought instead personal salvation in religion, philosophy and magic. The confident humanism of the fifth century B.C.E. gave way to a kind of resignation of man's fate to chance.

The new attitude was reflected in philosophy. Plato's Academy and Aristotle's Lyceum continued to be important, but changed somewhat in their emphases. Two new schools which offered ways of dealing with the insecurities of the times, however, flourished. Epicureanism sought not knowledge, but happiness, which the followers expected to find in a life based on reason. The Epicureans believed that true happiness depended on the avoidance of pain and advocated withdrawal from public life.

Stoicism was founded in Athens about 300 B.C.E. by Zeno of Cyprus. Their school advised men to live in harmony with God and nature by living in accordance with divine reason--a philosophy almost indistinguishable from religion. The wise Stoic knew what was good, what evil and what "indifferent." Above all, he avoided passion. Withdrawal was counseled, but duty was important and political activity allowed.

Perhaps the Hellenistic period's most lasting achievements were in mathematics and science, for they stood until the scientific revolution of the Renaissance. Euclid and Archimedes made great progress in geometry and physics; and the heliocentric and geocentric theories of planetary movement were both advocated and Eratosthenes offered a more detailed and accurate map of the world.

KEY POINTS AND VITAL CONCEPTS

1. <u>Development of the *Polis*</u>: The *polis* was an independent unit ruled by a variety of governments: monarchy, oligarchy, democracy, tyranny etc. In Athens, where the government progressed from monarchy to oligarchy to tyranny to democracy, the *polis* had an ethical purpose. As Aristotle noted, only in a *polis*, living under law, could man curb his baser instincts and fulfill his potential.

2. <u>The Tyrant</u>: It is important to remember that tyranny was not necessarily a pejorative form of government. Tyrants like Pisistratus often came to power, supported by hoplites (heavily-armed infantrymen) and discontented aristocrats. Tyrants often redistributed the land of the ruling aristocrats, encouraged trade, sponsored public works projects, introduced new festivals and patronized poets and artists. They usually promoted a policy of peace (for fear of having to arm the citizenry) with the result of prosperity for the people and popularity for the regime. By the end of the sixth century, however, the situation was reversed and the people of most *poleis* demanded a greater voice in government.

3. <u>Athenian Democracy</u>: It should be emphasized that Athenian democracy was truly "rule by the people" and each citizen had rights and responsibilities under law which demanded full participation in the government. Thucydides, the Athenian historian, later remarked that those people who kept to themselves and shirked their political responsibilities were worthless to the state. It is interesting that the Greek word for "private person," *idiotes*, would be transliterated as "idiot," with all its pejorative connotations. Athenian democracy, therefore, is very different from modern conceptions of democracy.

4. <u>The Athenian Empire</u>: There is a basic contradiction of principle in Athenian democracy. How can a state which espouses the freedom of democracy for all its citizens, maintain an empire of "allied states" by force? Since the great architecture and sculpture on the Acropolis were built under the direction of Pericles through funds demanded and collected by Athenian officials, the question then becomes: what price civilization? The Athenian empire can be seen as a fountain for Western Civilization or as an ethical contradiction. Without the funds contributed to Athens, could there have been such a flowering of art and culture in Athens?

5. <u>The Great Peloponnesian War</u>: This conflict has often been viewed as one war with three phases: 1) 431-421 B.C.E. 2) 421-415 B.C.E. 3) 415-404 B.C.E. Phases 1 and 3 were periods of "hot war". Phase 2 was one of "festering peace", as Thucydides termed it, where each side was suspicious and was moving for position before war would inevitably break out again. This is a pattern which repeats often in Western Civilization. Good examples might be the religious wars of the 16th, 17th and 18th centuries, as well as World Wars I and II which have been viewed as one war with a "festering peace" from 1919-1939.

6.   <u>The Hellenistic World</u>: The term "Hellenistic" was coined in the nineteenth century and means "Greek-like." It thus refers to a world which is similar to, but still distinct from, the Hellenic world of the Greeks in the fifth and fourth centuries. The new civilization was a mixture of Greek and Oriental elements, thanks in great part to the conquests of Alexander the Great. The Hellenistic world was much larger in area than the Hellenic world and its major units were much larger than city-states, though these persisted in different forms. It was a period of great political insecurity which in turn, inspired much important intellectual activity in mathematics, science and philosophy.

7.   <u>Alexander the Great</u>: Due to the paucity and exaggeration of our primary sources, the figure of Alexander remains an enigma to historians. For some, he represented an effort to unite East and West and to intermix races in hopes of establishing a "brotherhood of man". For others, Alexander was nothing more than a brutal, drunken egomaniac whose lust for conquest and glory overshadowed any other secondary achievements. The truth undoubtedly lies somewhere in between since we can never know his full intentions concerning his conquest. Perhaps Alexander himself did not fully plan or even comprehend the importance of his actions.

8.   <u>Greek and Hellenistic Civilization in World Perspective</u>: The striking thing about the emergence of Hellenic civilization is its sharp departure from the norm, rising as it did from a dark age in which a small number of poor, isolated and illiterate people developed their own kind of society. Political control was shared by a relatively large portion of the people and participation in political life was highly valued. Most states imposed no regular taxation, there was no separate caste of priests and little concern for life after death. Speculative natural philosophy based on observation and reason arose in this varied, dynamic, secular and remarkably free context. This was an era of unparalleled achievement. While the rest of the world continued to be characterized by monarchical, hierarchical command societies, Athenian democracy was carried as far as it would go before modern times. Democracy disappeared with the end of Greek autonomy late in the fourth century B.C.E. When it returned in the modern world more than two millennia later, it was broader but shallower, without the emphasis on active direct participation of every citizen in the government. In addition, many of the literary genres and forms that are ritual in the modern world arose and were developed during this time. The Greek emphasis on naturalistic art that idealized the human forms also diverged from previous and contemporary art in the rest of the world. To a great extent, these developments sprang from the independence and unique political experience of the Greeks.

IDENTIFICATION TERMS

For each of the following, tell who or what it is, about when did it happen, and why it is significant in the history of the period:

Cnossus (p. 78):

Homer (p. 80):

Salamis (p. 94):

Cimon (p. 96):

polis (p. 82):

hoplite (p. 82):

Philip of Macedon (p. 106):

Demosthenes (p. 106):

Zeno (p. 109):

League of Corinth (p. 107):

arete (p. 81):

Solon (p. 91):

helots (p. 89):

Epicurus (p. 109):

Clisthenes (p. 92):

MULTIPLE CHOICE QUESTIONS

1. The Minoan civilization was based on the
   - a. island of Crete
   - b. island of Thera
   - c. mainland of Greece
   - d. coast of Ionia

2. Which of the following is in the correct chronological order?
   - a. Minoan period, Mycenaean period, Dark Ages, Sack of Troy
   - b. Mycenaean period, Minoan period, Sack of Troy, Dark Ages
   - c. Minoan period, Mycenaean period, Sack of Troy, Dark Ages
   - d. Sack of Troy, Dark Ages, Minoan period, Mycenaean period

3. The highest virtue of an Homeric hero was
   - a. speed of foot
   - b. *agon* or desire
   - c. *arete* or courage
   - d. moral simplicity

4. Tyrants often came to power as a result of
   - a. an assassination of a political leader
   - b. a military defeat
   - c. a peasant rebellion
   - d. their military ability and support of the hoplites

5. Which of the following was a legacy of tyrants during the period 700-500 B.C.E.?
   - a. they temporarily put an end to civil wars
   - b. they reduced warfare between states
   - c. they encouraged progressive economic changes
   - d. all of the above

6. Which of the following was the location of the great Spartan defense of Greece against the Persians in 480 B.C.E.?
   - a. Thermopylae
   - b. Boeotia
   - c. Salamis
   - d. Marathon

7. The Delian League was transformed into the Athenian Empire because
   - a. of the pressure of war against Persia
   - b. of the rebellions of the Athenian allies
   - c. the allies were unwilling to see to their own defenses
   - d. all of the above

8. Women in Athens
    a. enjoyed full voting privileges
    b. were welcomed as important contributors to Athenian society and political life
    c. were excluded from most aspects of public life
    d. both a and b

9. The Athenian strategy during the opening phase of the Great Peloponnesian War was to
    a. allow the devastation of their land and rely on the income from their empire
    b. meet the Spartan army in battle
    c. force their allies to fight Sparta in pitched battle
    d. all of the above

10. The Sicilian expedition of 413 B.C.E. resulted in
    a. the rise to power of Alcibiades
    b. an Athenian victory
    c. the destruction of the entire Athenian force
    d. a Spartan alliance with Persia

11. Place these in the correct chronological order:
    a. Great Peloponnesian War, Spartan hegemony, Theban hegemony, Rise of Macedon
    b. Spartan hegemony, Great Peloponnesian War, Theban hegemony, Rise of Macedon
    c. Theban hegemony, Spartan hegemony, Rise of Macedon, Great Peloponnesian War
    d. Great Peloponnesian War, Theban hegemony, Spartan hegemony, Rise of Macedon

12. The leading Athenian spokesman against the encroachments of Philip of Macedon was
    a. Ephialtes   c. Isocrates
    b. Demosthenes   d. Darius

13. In 338 B.C.E. Philip settled his affairs in Greece by forming the
    a. Covenant of the Greeks   c. Chaeronean League
    b. Hegemony of Athens   d. Federal League of Corinth

14. After the death of Alexander in 323 B.C.E., his entire empire
    a. passed to the control of Ptolemy
    b. passed to the control of Seleucus
    c. broke apart into smaller parcels
    d. was conquered by the Medes

15. The Stoics
    a. sought the happiness of the individual
    b. believed that everyone had a spark of divinity in them
    c. were determined to lead the virtuous life
    d. all of the above

STUDY QUESTIONS

1. Who were the Minoans and Mycenaeans? What kinds of evidence about their civilizations do we possess? What was the relationship of Mycenaean to Minoan culture? Why did the Mycenaean civilization fail?

2. Compare and contrast the fundamental political, social and economic institutions of Athens and Sparta about 500 B.C.E. What were the major differences? Similarities?

3. Describe the workings of the system of government which Clisthenes created. What were its main features? What were the main changes from the previous system? What did the system mean to the common man?

4. Explain how the Athenian empire came into existence. Did it offer any advantages to its members? To what extent was the empire the basis for Athenian achievement in the fifth century and the basis for Athenian decline?

5. Why and how did Philip conquer Greece between 359 and 338 B.C.E.? How was he able to turn his region into a world power? Why did Demosthenes fail to defend Athens? Where does more of the credit for Philip's success lie: in Macedon's strength, or in Athens' weakness?

6. What were the major consequences of Alexander's death? Why did his empire fail to maintain political unity? Assess the achievement of Alexander. Was he a conscious promoter of Western Civilization or just an egomaniac drunk with the lust of conquest?

DOCUMENT QUESTIONS

1)   *Tyrtaeus Describes Excellence (p. 83):*

In this excerpt, how does Tyrtaeus define "excellence"? What are its components and how must a soldier attain it? What do these values say about Spartan society?

2)   *Hesiod's Farmer's Almanac (p. 87):*

After reading this excerpt from Hesiod's *Works and Days*, what do you think is the most important advice he offers? Why was farming so difficult in particular for a farmer cultivating land in Greece?

3)   *Athenian Democracy: An Unfriendly View (p. 99)*:

After reading this excerpt from an anonymous pamphleteer known as the "Old Oligarch," what are the author's objections to democracy? Does he describe the workings of Athenian democracy accurately? How would a defender of Athenian democracy counter his arguments?

4)   *Medea Bemoans the Condition of Women (p. 101)*:

What according to Euripides' account were some of the restrictions placed on women in Athenian society? How valid is it to speak of political and social freedom in Athenian society?

MAP ANALYSIS

Map 3-5: Classical Greece / Map 3-7: Alexander's Campaigns

Compare Map 3-5 on page 95 with that of 3-7 on page 102 of the textbook. Specifically, where and how did Alexander expand Greek influence beyond the Mediterranean? Do you think it valid that Alexander is often referred to as having "conquered the world"? How would the world be different had Alexander set out to conquer the West instead of the East?

MAP EXERCISE

Map 3-5: Classical Greece

Identify the following locations on Map 3-5 on page 95 of your textbook and place them on the map provided on the next page of this *Study Guide*.

1. Aegean Sea

2. Ionian Sea

3. Mediterranean Sea

4. Crete

5. Asia Minor

6. Macedonia

7. Athens

8. Sparta

9. Corinth

10. Delphi

11. Olympia

12. Megara

13. Argos

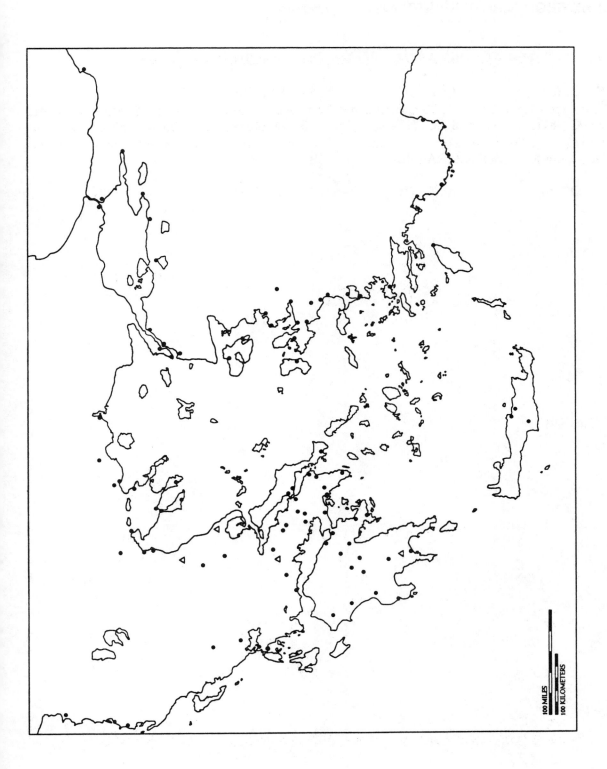

MAP 3-5
The Athenian Empire About 450 B.C.

MULTIPLE CHOICE ANSWER KEY *(with page references)*

1. A (78)	6. A (94)	11. A (101)
2. C (84)	7. D (94)	12. B (106)
3. C (81)	8. C (98)	13. D (107)
4. D (84)	9. A (100)	14. C (108)
5. D (86)	10. C (100)	15. D (109)

4

Iran, India and Inner Asia to 200 C.E.

COMMENTARY

This chapter continues the story of ancient civilization in Iran, inner Asia and the Indian subcontinent during the centuries surrounding the beginning of the Christian era. The chapter focuses on three major themes: 1) the rise of centralized empires on a new and unprecedented scale, 2) the increasing contact and interaction of major civilizations, and 3) the rise, spread and consolidation of major religious traditions that would have considerable effect on later history from Africa to China. The two most prominent peoples of the Iranian plateau were the Medes and Persians, who trace their ancestry back to the Vedic Age Indo-Aryans of north India. The Medes developed a tribal confederacy in western Iran that defeated the mighty Assyrian Empire in the late 7th century B.C.E. The rise of Persian power in the 7th and 6th centuries B.C.E., under the leadership of Cyrus the Great, led to the founding of the Achaemenid Empire.

Yet, the first person who stands out in Iranian history was not Cyrus, but Zarathustra, the great prophet reformer of Iranian religion. He is commonly known by the Greek version of his name, Zoroaster.

The rise of Iran as a world power and a major civilization dates from the reign of Cyrus the Great (559-530 B.C.E.). He ruled the Achaemenid clan in western Iran (Persis) and built his empire upon the gains of his grandfather, Cyrus I. Perhaps the greatest achievement of the Achaemenids was the stability of their rule. The empire was held together by a strong bureaucracy, a powerful military led by Persians, the universal sovereignty of the monarch and an advanced justice system. Provincial divisions, known as satrapies, maintained good roads and communications and gave the empire political unity in its cultural diversity. The Achaemenids were unable to expand their rule to the West and were defeated by the Greeks in 490 and 480 B.C.E. The final defeat of the empire came at the hands of Alexander the Great by 323 B.C.E.

The first Indian Empire (321-185 B.C.E.) developed on the plains of the Ganges River. It came only after the oriental campaigns of Alexander, who had conquered the Achaemenid provinces in the Indus Valley in 327 B.C.E. The first true Indian Empire was established by Chandrugupta Maurya (321-297 B.C.E.) as he captured lands to the west after Alexander's departure. The third and greatest Mauryan emperor, Ashoka (ca. 272-232 B.C.E.), left numerous rock inscriptions that note his conquests of Kalinga and the Deccan, thus extending Mauryan control over the whole subcontinent, except the far south. After that, Ashoka underwent a religious conversion and championed nonviolence (*ahimsa*) and the ideal of "conquest by righteousness" (*dharma*).

The post-Mauryan period saw Buddhist monasticism and lay devotionalism thrive throughout the sub-continent. What we now call Hinduism also emerged in this era with the consolidation of the caste system, Brahman ascendancy and the "high culture" of Sanskrit language and learning. A certain merging of Buddhist and Hindu ideas gave both religious groups a dynamic aspect in later periods.

The Seleucid successors to Alexander the Great maintained their power in Iran through mercenary troops and never secured lasting rule on the scale of the Achaemenids. In the end, Alexander's policy of linking Hellenes with Iranians in political power, marriage and culture bore more lasting fruit than empire.

The Parthians succeeded the Seleucids in Iran and continued their rule from about 250 B.C.E. to 300 C.E. Their most famous ruler, Mithradates I (171-138 B.C.E.), was able to secure a sizeable empire, one that threatened Rome from 53 B.C.E. In the end, the pressure of the Kushan empire in the east and above all, the Roman wars of the third century weakened the Parthians enough for a new Persian dynasty to replace them. The Sakas and Kushans played an important role in cultural diffusion from this area, and were responsible for the missionary activity that carried Buddhism across the steppes into China.

This was also an era in which influential lasting religious traditions (Christian, Buddhist, Confucian, Judaic and Hindu) came of age and spread in cultures outside their places of origin. This period also saw increased cross-cultural development, demonstrated by the Hellenizing conquests of Alexander the Great. Although African cultures lagged behind development in the West and East, this was due primarily to their relative isolation, rather than to the character of their peoples.

KEY POINTS AND VITAL CONCEPTS

1. Zoroastrianism: The evolution of the Zoroastrian faith was part of the older Iranian culture and religion associated with the Vedic Aryans. Zarathustra (628-551 B.C.E.) was the leader of this movement and preached a message of moral reform in an age when materialism, political opportunism and ethical indifference were common. Zoroastrianism probably influenced not only the Jewish, Christian and Muslim ideas of the Messiah, angels, devils, the last judgment, and an afterlife, but also certain Buddhist concepts as well. It was wiped out as a major force by Islam in the 7th and 8th centuries C.E., but its tradition continues in the faith and practice of the Parsis in western India.

2. Indo-Iranian Empires: The Achaemenids, Mauryans, Parthians, Sakas and Kushans developed similar characteristics of complex empires. These included good administration, professional armies, effective communications and stability. These developments created opportunities for interaction between China and the Greek worlds through Buddhism and increased trade. The contributions of these empires created a dynamic opportunity for the Steppe people to influence humankind. The assimilation of various cultures created a "high culture" in India of lasting importance.

3. The Merging of Cultures: Because of imperial development during this period, two distinct cultures merged together: Mesopotamia and Iran, and the subcontinent of India. Thus Central Asia remained a cultural melting pot with cross-cultural contacts that affected the Mediterranean, Western Eurasia, India and China. These contributions included steppe-nomad languages, arts, religious practices and techniques of government. Even though the Iranian and Indian cultures remained distinct, the development of contacts had a lasting impact on humankind.

IDENTIFICATION TERMS

For each of the following, tell who or what it is, about when did it happen, and why it is significant in the history of the period:

Satrap (p. 122):

Arthashastra (p. 126):

Chandragupta (p. 125):

Asha (p. 120):

Deccan (p. 126):

Dharma (p. 126):

Magi (p. 120):

Ahimsa (p. 126):

Scythians (p. 121):

Achaemenid (p. 120):

Cyrus the Great (p. 120):

Pahlavas (p. 133):

Shahanshah (p. 121):

Sanskrit (p. 129):

Zoroaster (p. 119):

MULTIPLE CHOICE QUESTIONS

1. The most prominent of the Iranian peoples were
   a. Bactrians
   b. Persians
   c. Medes
   d. both b and c

2. *Asha* can best be defined as
   a. "Wise Lord"
   b. "Lie"
   c. "Truth" or "Right"
   d. "Great Prophet"

3. The first person who stand out in Iranian history was
   a. Cyrus
   b. Cambyses
   c. Zarathustra
   d. Darius

4. Zoroaster (628-551 B.C.E.) preached a message similar to all of the following <u>except</u>:
   a. Hebrew Prophets
   b. Democritus
   c. Buddha
   d. Confucius

5. Zoroaster called on people to
   a. abandon worship of Ahura Mazda
   b. destroy the priestly clan known as the *Magi*
   c. turn from the "Lie" (*druj*) to the "Truth" (*asha*)
   d. all of the above

6. Which of the following served as the capital of Persia
   a. Babylon
   b. Ecbatana
   c. Susa/Persepolis/Parsargadae
   d. all of the above

7. Under the reign of the Persian king, Darius,
   a. the Greeks defeated the Persians
   b. Greece was added to the empire
   c. Egypt was added to the empire
   d. the advance of the Scythians was halted

8. Much of the Achaemenid administrative success lay in their
   a. tribal confederation
   b. willingness to learn and borrow from predecessors
   c. military despotism
   d. forced conversion to the state religious cult

9. Kautilya, the *Brahman* minister to Chandragupta was also known as
    a. the "Great Adventurer"
    b. Arthashastra
    c. the "Indian Machiavelli"
    d. the "Divine Wind"

10. *Dharma* can best be defined as
    a. nonviolence   c. "conquest by righteousness"
    b. "life-blood"   d. "holy war"

11. Mauryan bureaucracy was marked by
    a. centralization   c. a secret service
    b. corruption   d. both a and c

12. Two masterpieces of Sanskrit culture around 200 C.E. were
    a. *Shiva and Vishnu*   c. *Arthashastra and Shahanshah*
    b. *Mahabharata and Ramayana*   d. *Asha and Gathas*

13. A primary reason that Buddhism remained only one among many Indian religious paths was
    a. that it was absorbed into the diversity that typifies the Hindu religious scene
    b. the fact most people could not read the Buddhist religious tracts
    c. that Buddhist saints were never identified with popular Indian deities
    d. that lay people could not spend the time trying to attain *nirvana* as could Buddhist monks

14. Culturally, the Parthians were oriented toward the Hellenistic world until the mid-first century C.E. when they were influenced by
    a. Iranian art motifs   c. the Greek alphabet
    b. Roman statuary   d. commerce with China

15. In the first century B.C.E. the Sakas were defeated in northwestern India by the
    a. Yueh Chih from the steppes of China   c. Jaxartes and his pirate raiders
    b. Bactrian Greeks from the west   d. *Pahlavas* invading from Iran

STUDY QUESTIONS

1. How did Mauryan organization affect communication and the rise of urban centers? Why was Ashoka's conversion to Buddhism important in the creation of the Mauryan empire? What were some of the policies effected by Ashoka? Discuss the Mauryan legacy in world history.

2. How did the Achaemenid state rule over a long period of time? What were the main aspects of government control that enhanced the power base? What was the role of the religion in this development?

3. How was the first great Indian Empire created? What role did Chandragupta have in this movement? What geographic hurdles had to be overcome to bring the empire together? Why was the interaction with the Greeks important in this development?

4. Discuss the major features of the Hindu and Buddhist traditions. What are the similarities between the two groups? Why did Buddhism spread to China and southeast Asia while Hinduism remained in India?

5. Describe the effect Hellenistic culture had on the Seleucid rule. How were their concepts different from those of Alexander the Great? What were the major contributions of the Greek world to the East and what was the specific effect on Bactria?

6. What major role did the Steppe people play in the Eurasian subcontinent? How did the Parthians control a vast area with only a limited culture? What were the major differences between the rule of the Sakas and Kushans, and the Parthians? In what ways can the Kushans and Sakas be considered important to world history?

DOCUMENT QUESTIONS

1) *A Hymn of Zoroaster (p. 119):*

According to this selection, what kind of a struggle is occurring on the divine level? Which path does the "most Holy Spirit" take? How do you define "dualism" and what meaning does this divine struggle have on a human level?

2) *Building the Royal Palace at Susa (p. 124):*

After reading this document, which of the many accomplishments of Darius do you think is the most impressive? How specifically does this inscription demonstrate the extent of Achaemenid power and dominion?

3) *Darius on the Throne (p. 123):*

Look carefully at this relief from Persepolis. What does it tell you about the Persian government and position of the king? Be specific in your analysis.

4) *The Edicts of Ashoka (p. 127):*

Compare the Edicts of Ashoka with the inscriptions noting the accomplishments of Darius on page 212 of your textbook. How is power and righteousness demonstrated in the Edicts of Ashoka? What is the "universal conquest" that is mentioned in the Thirteenth Rock Edict?

MAP ANALYSIS

Map 4-1: The Achaemenid Persian Empire

Compare the extent of the Persian Empire as depicted in Map 4-1 on page 121 of the textbook with Alexander's Empire (Map 3-7, page 102) and the Roman Empire (Map 5-4, page 158). List these empires in chronological order. What similarities and differences do you see in the borders and extent of these empires? Which peoples were the most efficient organizers of empire and how did they accomplish this?

MAP EXERCISE

Map 4-1: The Achaemenid Persian Empire

The Achaemenid Empire touched all of these bodies of water. Locate them on the map on page 121 of your textbook and copy them onto the map on the next page of this *Study Guide*:

1. Black Sea   5. Red Sea

2. Caspian Sea   6. Mediterranean Sea

3. Aral Sea   7. Aegean Sea

4. Persian Gulf

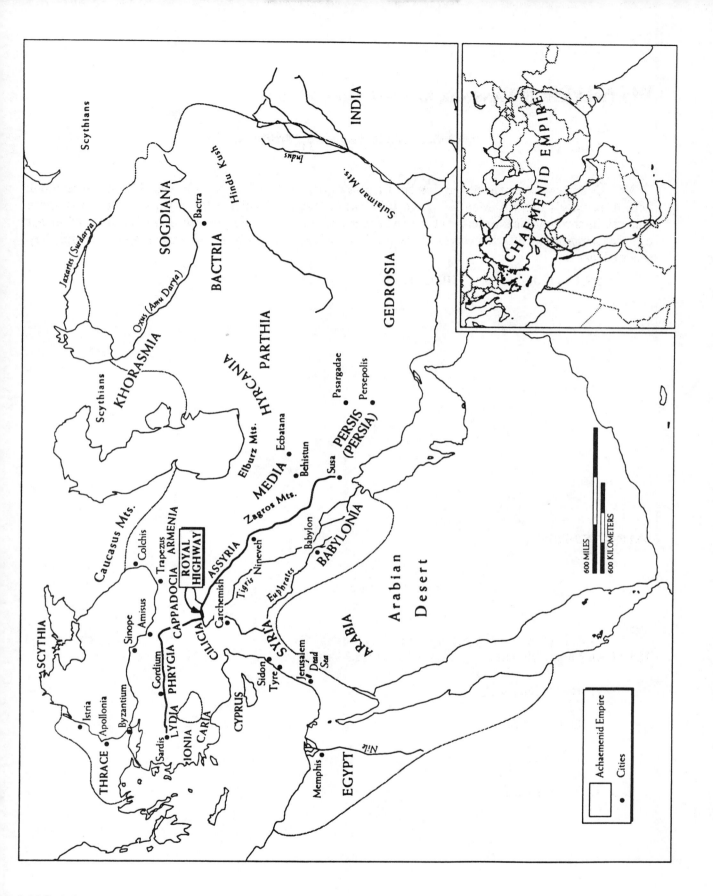

MAP 4-1
The Achaemenid Persian Empire

MULTIPLE CHOICE ANSWER KEY *(with page references)*

1. D (118)	6. D (120)	11. D (128)
2. C (119)	7. A (121)	12. B (129)
3. C (119)	8. B (122)	13. A (130)
4. B (119)	9. C (126)	14. A (132)
5. C (120)	10. C (126)	15. D (133)

5
Republican and Imperial Rome

COMMENTARY

After describing Italy before the rise of Rome, the society of royal Rome, and the early republic and its constitution, this chapter tells the story of Rome's expansion: the conquest of Italy, the wars with Carthage, the increasing involvement with the Greek world, the eventual takeover of the Hellenistic east, and finally the decline of the republic amid political factions and civil war, the Augustan settlement, the prosperity, decline, and fall of the Roman Empire.

Civilized Etruscans arrived in Tuscany (Etruria), perhaps from the east, about 800 B.C.E. and established themselves in a loose corporation of self-governing city-states. The Etruscans dominated the native Italians and accumulated considerable wealth. They expanded both to the north and south, but their conquests were not firmly based and were lost in the course of the fifth century B.C.E. However, Etruscan influence on the Romans remained particularly in religion.

The chapter goes on to describe Roman society and government under the kings (753-509 B.C.E.). In essence, Rome was ruled by a king whose powers were limited by his advisors, who composed the Senate, and an assembly of the people.

The center of Roman life was the family, in which the father had a position analogous to that of the king in the state. One of Rome's most important institutions was clientage; a client entrusted himself to the protection of a more powerful man (called a patron) in exchange for services which included military and political support.

A revolution in 509 B.C.E. replaced the monarchy with the republic. Early Roman society had a class distinction based on birth: the patricians monopolized the positions of power and influence while the plebeians were barred from public office and from the priesthoods. Over the next two centuries they tried to achieve equality with the patricians. Their attempt was called the "struggle of the orders" and by 287 B.C.E., through legal means, the plebeians gained full access to the magistracies, as well as an important voice in the government. But still only a small group of leading families dominated the Senate and highest magistracies.

Rome's conquest of Italy took more than two centuries. The Romans dealt with conquered cities quite liberally, offering citizenship to some, potential citizenship to others and allied status to the rest. By the middle of the third century, Rome had consolidated her Italian gains and came face to face with Carthage, the great naval power of the western Mediterranean. Rome fought three major wars against Carthage from 264-241; 218-201; and 149-146 B.C.E. Roman resources and fortitude were taxed to the limit, especially in the Second Punic War against the great general Hannibal; but in the end, Carthage was completely destroyed.

Rome's victory against Carthage and her success in the eastern Mediterranean against Macedonia and Antiochus III in Asia Minor from about 215-150, opened the way to Roman supervision of the entire

Mediterranean region. Such was not an easy task. Greeks and Romans did not understand freedom in the same way. The Romans found themselves becoming more and more involved in the affairs of Greece and Asia. Anti-Roman factions in the Greek cities were punished severely. Whether intended or not, Rome's expansion brought with it power, wealth and responsibility. The Roman constitution which had been well adapted to the mastery of Italy would be severely tested by the need to govern an empire beyond the seas.

By the middle of the second century B.C.E., Rome faced a serious manpower problem: peasants were losing their land and many could no longer qualify for the army. A political threat was also developing, as patrons had less control over clients who fled their land. In 133 B.C.E. a young tribune from an aristocratic family, Tiberius Gracchus, attempted to solve these problems by proposing that public land be redistributed to the poor. The bill aroused great hostility and after untraditional and unprecedented, but not illegal measures by Tiberius to pass the bill, he was murdered by a mob of senators and their clients. Nevertheless, his career brought a permanent change to Roman politics as he showed an alternative to the traditional aristocratic career: politicians could go directly to the people.

In 123 B.C.E. Tiberius' younger brother, Gaius, became tribune with a much broader platform of reforms, designed to appeal to a variety of groups. Of primary importance was his insistence that full Roman citizenship be offered to the Italian allies. This proposal failed and after he lost a bid for reelection, Gaius also was hunted down and killed under sanction of a senatorial decree.

After the revolt of the frustrated Italian allies in 90 B.C.E. and the subsequent "social war," Rome offered them full citizenship. A successful general in the war, Sulla, dominated the next decade as he became consul and tried to restore senatorial government by reconstituting the state and restricting the powers of the people and their representatives, the tribunes.

The chapter recounts in detail the rise of Pompey and Crassus in the 70s and 60s B.C.E. Crassus was responsible for the suppression of the slave revolt of Spartacus in 73 B.C.E. and Pompey received extraordinary commands against the pirates and Mithradates. Always successful, Pompey had to share some of his glory with the great orator, Cicero, who as consul in 63 B.C.E., had saved the state from the conspiracy of Catiline. The decade of the 60s also saw the rise of Julius Caesar who combined with Pompey and Crassus in 60 B.C.E. to control the state in an association termed the "first triumvirate."

The decade of the 50's saw the death of Crassus and the polarization of Caesar and Pompey. Their coalition fell apart with Pompey supporting the senate against Caesar. In 49 B.C.E. Caesar led his troops across the Rubicon River starting a civil war which ended in 46 B.C.E. with Caesar the victor.

In the years before his death, Caesar did not spend much time in Rome. It is hard to be sure what reorganization of the state he had in mind, but he seems to have had a moderate and sensible approach to problems. On March 15, 44 B.C.E., however, Caesar was assassinated by Brutus, Cassius and other senators who hoped to restore the republic, but succeeded only in unleashing thirteen more years of civil war, after which the republic was forever dead.

The period from 44-31 B.C.E. saw the duel between Caesar's lieutenant, Mark Antony, and his eighteen year old heir, Octavian. After some pretence at cooperation, Antony chose the wealth of the east and the alliance of Cleopatra; Octavian chose the west as his power base. Octavian won a decisive victory at Actium in 31 B.C.E. which was soon followed by the suicides of Antony and Cleopatra. At the age of thirty-two, Octavian was absolute master of the Mediterranean world.

Octavian was determined to avoid the fate of Julius Caesar. He gradually developed a system which left most of the real power to himself but pretended to be a restoration of the republic with Octavian as *princeps* ("first citizen"). The governmental system of the early Roman Empire is thus called the principate. The settlement of Augustus (as he was now called) was able to enlist the support of the upper classes. The Senate elected magistrates, made laws and exercised important judicial functions.

These powers were, nevertheless, illusory in that the Senate merely assented to candidates or laws placed before it by the emperor. Opposition to imperial rule did exist especially under such emperors as Caligula, Nero and Domitian who failed to play the game well and did not respect the dignity or property of the senators. Under Augustus, Tiberius, Claudius, Vespasian, Titus and the five "good emperors," however, the empire was run well and the *Pax Romana* (Roman Peace) was maintained throughout the empire.

Roman culture was at its height during this time. The chapter goes on to discuss the great literary figures of the late republic such as Cicero, Sallust, Caesar, Lucretius and Catullus. The patronage of Augustus played an important role in the manufacture of propaganda as well as great literature in the works of Livy, Horace and Vergil, whose epic poem, the *Aeneid*, portrayed Augustus as the second founder of Rome. Roman architects kept the basic construction techniques of the Greeks, but developed a semi-circular arch and concrete with which they were able to build structures of great size: the Colosseum, the baths and the Pantheon. Roman sculptors specialized in the reliefs found on columns.

The growth of Christianity is also recounted as is the decline and fall of the Roman Empire. The period from 235-285 was one of political chaos which saw twenty-six recognized rulers with only one dying a natural death. With a new defense strategy which included an emphasis on heavy cavalry and a mobile army as well as fortified cities, the Romans were able to check barbarian threats. The army, however, was now composed largely of mercenaries only technically Roman; the Romans hired barbarians to protect them from barbarians.

Reconstruction and reorganization took place under Diocletian (285-305) and Constantine (324-337). Diocletian introduced the tetrarchy, under which the empire was divided into parts and ruled by two senior Augusti and two junior Caesars who were to succeed the Augusti. This plan for better administration and smooth succession failed as a civil war erupted after Diocletian's retirement in 305. By 324, the empire was united again by Constantine who built the new capital of Constantinople on the site of ancient Byzantium. Under Diocletian and Constantine, the emperor changed from *princeps* (first citizen) to *dominus* (lord); hence the system of government was called the dominate. The emperor ruled by decree; the Senate had no role whatever. The economic reforms of Diocletian were unsuccessful and inflation was rampant although alleviated somewhat by Constantine. Stern regimentation was necessary to keep everyone in their occupations in order to assure stable production.

Renewed barbarian invasions in the fifth century put an end to effective imperial government in the west. Soil exhaustion, plague, climatic change and even lead poisoning have been suggested as reasons for Rome's decline in manpower. Slavery has been blamed for preventing scientific and technological advances. Some blame excessive governmental interference in the economic life of the empire, while others look to the destruction of the urban middle class.

We would do better to try to understand why the empire survived so long. Rome expanded to the limits of her ability to conquer and to govern. Without new conquests to provide the immense wealth needed for defense and maintenance of internal prosperity, the Romans yielded to unprecedented onslaughts by fierce and numerous attackers. When we contemplate the decline and fall of the Roman Empire in the fourth and fifth centuries, we are only speaking of the west. A form of classical culture persisted in the east, centered in Constantinople. The Byzantine Empire would last until the fifteenth century.

KEY POINTS AND VITAL CONCEPTS

1.   Roman Constitution: One of the great achievements of the Romans was their constitution. An unwritten collection of laws based upon tradition and precedent, it sanctioned a government dependent upon two principles: annuality and collegiality. That is, more than one person held each office (with the exception of the dictatorship) and they held it generally for one year only. Each citizen was allowed to vote and did in a number of traditional assemblies. Intended to govern a city-state, the constitution was appended to meet the demands of imperial administration.

2.   Struggle of the Orders: The period from 509 to 207 B,C, has been termed the "Struggle of the Orders" since the plebeians agitated for legal equality with the patricians. Gradually the plebeians, through tactics such as secession, won full legal, political and social equality with the patricians. This was achieved without bloodshed - a point which the Romans were proud of and which contrasted with the chaos and violence of the late republic.

3.   Roman Imperialism: A much debated point in Roman history concerns Roman intentions in the acquisition of her empire. Did Rome have a blueprint for empire and consciously follow a policy of aggressive imperialism? The answer is probably no, but once Rome became involved in a dispute (especially in the Greek east and often by invitation), she found it difficult to remain neutral with her own interests and even survival at stake. Within about 120 years, Rome had expanded from control of the Italian peninsula to mastery of the entire Mediterranean - a transformation which would present great problems for the state in the second and first centuries B.C.E.

4.   The Reforms of the Gracchi: The reforms instituted by the Gracchi which included redistribution of public land, colonies, Italian citizenship, subsidized grain, etc., were not illegal and in some cases even had precedent. Yet it was their method, especially that of Tiberius, which aroused the hatred of the aristocracy. Many precedents for later actions proceeded from the Gracchan episode, including murder and violent intimidation sanctioned by a dubious enactment called the "Final Decree of the Senate." A major problem which was not solved during this period was the approval of Italian citizenship. In the end, Rome would fight the Social War (90-88 B.C.E.) and win, only to agree to full Italian citizenship anyway.

5.   The Augustan Principate: The Augustan settlement ostensibly restored the republic, but in fact established a monarchy. Augustus controlled twenty of the twenty-six legions in the provinces with the most potential for fighting. Egypt with its wealth and important grain production belonged to him alone. In fact, geographically the imperial provinces practically surrounded the senatorial. However, Augustus knew that he could not rule by force alone. He built around him a coalition of supporters who owed their positions to him. Augustus respected the dignity of the senators by using them in the administration and listening to their advice. This "sham of government," as it has been called, put a premium upon efficient and equitable treatment of its citizens. The strength of the system can be evaluated in its survival even through the reigns of incompetent and cruel emperors.

6. The Displacement of Rome as Capital of the Empire: In accordance with Diocletian's reorganization of government, the empire was divided into four parts for better defense and administration. It is significant that Diocletian chose Nicomedia in the east as his center of administration. The advantages of an eastern capital were overwhelming: greater wealth, population, and tax base as well as freedom from the more intense barbarian activity of the west. Constantine formally moved the capital from Rome to Constantinople, a city which was set in a perfect geographic location for defense and control of the eastern trade. The Byzantine Empire, centered there, would last until the fifteenth century.

7. The Success of Christianity: Christianity had many philosophies and mystery religions to compete with beyond the pagan gods. Why was Christianity successful in the end? A few suggestions: A) Christianity was not exclusive, appealing to rich and poor, male and female, children and adults of whatever race B) Christianity was a missionary religion which took advantage of Roman roads and the Roman peace C) It espoused a philosophy of love and sacrifice told in parables which were easy to understand D) It won over members of the intellectual upper class through apologies by Jerome, Tertullian and Augustine, as well as through doctrine defined by Clement, Origen and others E) It existed early in the shadow of Judaism, a religion with special privileges under Roman law, and thus was somewhat protected F) It was persecuted which added to its appeal, since people were willing to die for beliefs which therefore must be valid G) The threat and existence of heresies (Arianism) demanded a close evaluation and strengthened doctrine H) It offered a life after death for true believers I) With the support of the emperor Constantine, its existence was assured. Many other cults offered some of these benefits, but the attraction of Christianity was formidable.

8. Republican and Imperial Rome in World Perspective: The history of the Republic is a sharp departure from the common experience of ancient civilizations. In the development from a monarchy to a republic founded on equitable laws, and the subsequent accumulation and administration of empire, the Romans displayed their pragmatic character. They created something unique: an empire ruled by elected magistrates with an effective power equal to the kings and emperors of China, India and Iran. However, the temptations and responsibilities of such a vast empire proved too much for the republican constitution. The influx of slaves led to the displacement of citizens, who served as professional soldiers in the service of generals seeking personal glory above loyalty to the state. The conquest of a vast empire led the Romans toward the more familiar path of development experienced by rulers in Egypt, Mesopotamia, China, India and Iran. Comparisons can be made with the Chinese "dynastic cycle" that included a period of strength and security fortified by impressive leadership. Like the former Han Dynasty in China, the Roman Empire in the west fell, leaving disunity, insecurity, disorder and poverty. Like similar empires in the ancient world, it had been unable to sustain its "immoderate greatness."

IDENTIFICATION TERMS

For each of the following, tell who or what it is, about when did it happen, and why it is significant in the history of the period:

princeps (p. 155):

Trajan (p. 160):

plebeian (p. 141):

consul (p. 141):

Virgil (p. 156):

Hannibal (p. 144):

Paul of Tarsus (p. 163):

Arianism (p. 170):

"five good emperors" (p. 159):

Tiberius Gracchus (p. 151):

Dominus (p. 167):

Edict of Maximum Prices (p. 168):

First Triumvirate (p. 153):

Pompey (p. 153):

Crassus (p. 153):

MULTIPLE CHOICE QUESTIONS

1. *Imperium* can best be defined as the
   a. right to issue and enforce commands
   b. right to collect taxes
   c. right of property
   d. none of the above

2. The Roman woman
   a. could be sold or killed by her husband
   b. enjoyed a respected position in the family and ran the household
   c. was the chief priest of the family
   d. could vote in the assembly

3. In Rome, the patron-client relationship was
   a. based on fear of one for the other
   b. based on heredity
   c. sanctioned by religion and custom
   d. both b and c

4. The Roman constitution was
   a. an unwritten accumulation of laws and customs
   b. a written document kept under the strictest security
   c. a compiled record of several Italian constitutions
   d. both a and c

5. The Struggle of the Orders
   a. was a patrician campaign to achieve political, legal and social equality
   b. resulted in the fall of the Roman Republic
   c. resulted in the decline of the senate
   d. none of the above

6. The tribunate of Tiberius Gracchus proved that a Roman could
   a. pursue a political career that was not based solely on influence within the aristocracy
   b. appeal to the popular will of the people for influence
   c. no longer ignore the power of the senate
   d. both a and b

7. The First Triumvirate consisted of
   a. Pompey, Caesar, and Sulla
   b. Caesar, Crassus, and Marius
   c. Pompey, Caesar, and Crassus
   d. Marius, Sulla, and Pompey

8. Caesar established his fame as a general by
    a. defeating Spartacus
    c. conquering Gaul
    b. destroying Octavian
    d. saving Rome from Catiline

9. Augustus was successful in making the transition from a republican government because he
    a. emphasized his military power
    b. maintained the appearance of republican institutions and masked the monarchical reality
    c. eliminated all of his rivals
    d. emphasized his unprecedented powers and disregarded republican traditions

10. During his lifetime, Augustus
    a. accepted divine honors
    b. introduced foreign gods into the Roman cults
    c. repealed legislation curbing divorce and adultery
    d. none of the above

11. The poets Virgil and Horace were
    a. patronized by Augustus
    b. executed by Augustus
    c. mere propagandists
    d. exiled to the Black Sea region for displeasing Augustus

12. The peaceful accession of adoptive emperors ended
    a. with the assassination of Domitian
    b. when Marcus Aurelius' son, Commodus, ascended to the throne
    c. when Nerva chose the warlike Trajan as his successor
    d. when Caligula was assassinated

13. The main contribution of the Romans to architecture lay in
    a. their use of marble
    b. the great size of structures they could build because of engineering advancements
    c. their extreme attention to detail especially in reducing the scale of buildings
    d. their attention to religious structures

14. Most persecutions of Christians were instituted by
    a. mob action
    c. the Jewish Pharisees
    b. the Roman government
    d. orthodox Greeks

15. The Council of Nicea in 325,
    a. affirmed that Arianism was the accepted doctrine of the Christian Church
    b. sought to define the nature of the Trinity
    c. was called by the Emperor Constantine
    d. both b and c

STUDY QUESTIONS

1.   What was the "struggle of the orders"? What did the plebeians want? What methods did they use to get what they wanted? To what degree was Roman society different after the struggle ended?

2.   Explain the causes of the clash between the Romans and the Carthaginians in the First and Second Punic Wars. Could the wars have been averted? Who bears the ultimate responsibility?

3.   What domestic problems did Italy have in the middle of the second century B.C.E.? What caused these problems? What were the main proposals of Tiberius and Gaius Gracchus? Why did they fail? What other questions about Roman domestic policy had the Gracchi raised through their deaths?

4.   Why was the Roman population willing to accept Augustus as head of the state? What answers did Augustus provide for the problems which had plagued the republic? Describe the Augustan settlement of government. In what manner did Augustus rule?

5.   In spite of unpromising beginnings, Christianity was enormously successful by the fourth century C.E.   Who were its competitors? What were the more important reasons which help explain its success?

6.   In recent years, a number of persons have said that they see in the United States the same forces at work that caused the decline of the Roman Empire. Do you find this idea convincing? What are the components of decline? Is the decline of each civilization inevitable?

DOCUMENT QUESTIONS

1)   *A Woman's Uprising in Republican Rome (p. 146)*:

According to Livy's account, why were the women upset? How did they try to achieve their goals and what were Cato's specific objections? What does this incident say about the relative political power of women in Rome?

2)   *The Ruin of the Family Farm and the Gracchan Reforms (p. 152)*:

According to Plutarch, what were the specific problems faced by Roman farmers? What solution did Tiberius Gracchus propose and why was it considered to be so radical?

3) *Daily Life in a Roman Provincial Town: Graffiti from Pompeii (p. 160)*:

What do these graffiti from the walls of ancient Pompeii tell you about life in that town? How different are the desires and interests of ancient Romans from those of modern city dwellers?

4) *Mark Describes the Resurrection of Jesus (p. 164):*

What is the symbolism associated with the resurrection of Jesus? Why is the idea of resurrection and salvation such a popular component of Christianity?

MAP ANALYSIS

Map 5-5: Divisions of the Roman Empire Under Diocletian

Analyze the divisions of the Roman empire in Map 5-5 on page 168 of your textbook. Why was the empire divided into four areas and why specifically <u>these</u> four divisions? Which area would you have preferred to rule and why?

MAP EXERCISE

Map 5-3: Roman Dominions of the Late Republic

By the time of Julius Caesar's death, Roman domination had spread across the Mediterranean from Iberia to Asia and part of Africa. Identify the following locations on Map 5-3 on page 149 of your textbook and place them on the map provided on the next page of this *Study Guide*.

1. Rome	10. Sicily
2. Italy	11. Illyricum
3. Mauretania (client kingdom)	12. Asia
4. Thrace (client kingdom)	13. Macedon
5. Palestine	14. Cilicia
6. Armenia	15. Cyprus
7. Gaul	16. Crete
8. Corsica	17. Achaea
9. Sardinia	18. Spain

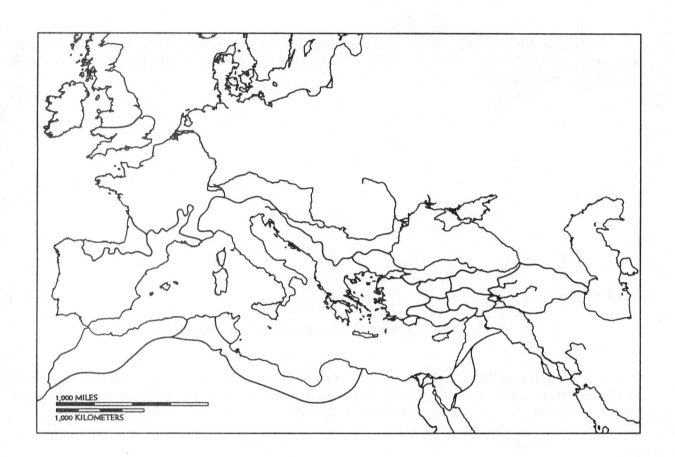

MAP 5-3
Roman Dominions of the Late Republic

MULTIPLE CHOICE ANSWER KEY *(with page references)*

1. A (140)	6. D (151)	11. A (157)
2. B (141)	7. C (153)	12. B (159)
3. D (141)	8. C (154)	13. B (161)
4. A (141)	9. B (155)	14. A (165)
5. D (142)	10. D (155)	15. D (170)

6
Africa: Early History to 1000 C.E.

COMMENTARY

The chapter begins with an introduction to the continent of Africa, noting particularly its geographical divisions, natural resources and trade links to Europe and Asia. Despite natural barriers, Africa's peoples have not been as internally isolated or compartmentalized as was once thought. Unlike other continents, African history has not been one of major empires and a few primary centers of cultural diffusion. The chief cause of this was the increasing desiccation of the northern third of the continent. In the first millennium B.C.E., negroid peoples of the Sudan developed and refined techniques for agriculture; as early as 500 B.C.E., the Nok culture had entered the Iron Age.

Perhaps the most important and impressive of the early African kingdoms was located in the upper Nile basin, in lower Nubia. The kingdom of Kush became the successor to the Egyptian empire and was first centered in the city of Napata (10th century B.C.E.) and later in Meroe during the 6th century B.C.E. This Meroitic empire enjoyed a long and prosperous life before it began to decline about 100 C.E. with its final collapse at the end of the 4th century C.E.

The chapter then focuses on the Aksumite Empire which succeeded the Kushite about 330 C.E. The newly Christianized state of Aksum was located to the south of Kush and was a product of a linguistic, cultural and genetic mixing of African Kushitic speakers with Semitic speakers from southern Arabia. By the first century C.E., its chief port of Adulis had become the major ivory and elephant market of northeastern Africa. By the third century C.E., Aksum was one of the most impressive states of its age in the African or western Asian world, as the remains of the imposing stone buildings and monuments of its major cities testify. The Aksumites enjoyed relatively cordial relations with the new Muslim domains to the north in Egypt and across the Red Sea during the seventh and eighth centuries C.E. Incursions of the Muslim Mamluk rulers of Egypt in the fourteenth and fifteenth centuries led ultimately to the Islamization and conversion of the whole Nubian region. Ethiopia was left as the sole predominantly Christian state in Africa.

The peoples of the Western and Central Sudan form the next section of the text. The first millennium C.E. saw the growth of settled agricultural populations and the development and expansion of trans-Saharan and other internal trade. These developments coincided with the rise of several sizable states in the western and central Sudan, among them Takrur, Ghana, Gao, and Kanem.

Available sources have made it difficult to reconstruct the history of Central, Southern, and East Africa. The two groups that collectively constitute the Khoisan speakers are the San ("Bushmen") and the Khoikhoi (the "Hottentots" of older European usage). Recent research has challenged the notion that the Khoikhoi were generally herdsmen and the San were hunter-gatherers. Scholars have argued that a great deal of the common wisdom concerning these peoples is the result of colonialist and post-colonialist prejudice against them. The chapter then focuses on the diffusion of speakers of the Bantu language group and then centers on the overseas trade of the East Africa peoples. This included exports of ivory to Greece, India, and China, as well as wood, food grains, slaves and gold in Islamic times. Migrations from the north and West to the eastern highlands over many centuries have made the highlands a melting pot of Kushitic, Nilotic, Bantu, and Khosisan groups We see the radical diversity of peoples and cultures of the entire continent mirrored in the heritages of a single major region.

KEY POINTS AND VITAL CONCEPTS

1. The Question of "Civilization": The term, *civilization*, has a broader meaning than that offered in Chapter 1 of a cluster of attributes (writing, urban life, and metallurgy) that relate to social complexity and technological development. Some have associated the term *civilization* with a people's cultural and artistic traditions and sophistication. The two meanings are often confused, leading to unfortunate assumptions that societies without writing, cities, or a state bureaucracy are "uncivilized" in a broader sense. African history includes important states with all of the mentioned characteristics, but also many societies with rich and varied traditions that did not happen to be organized into bureaucratic states with literate, urban populations and advanced technology. This does not make them any less civilized in the broader context.

2. Africa and Early Human Culture: Recent archeological research indicates that our hominid ancestor evolved in the Great Rift region of highland East Africa perhaps earlier than 1.8 million years ago. It was also here that modern human species (*homo sapiens*) appeared sometime before 100,000 B.C.E. The popular view coming out of the nineteenth century that Africa south of the Sahara was a vast region isolated from civilization until it was "discovered" by Europeans badly distorts reality and contributes to prejudices that Europeans "civilized" the African continent. African goods were for centuries in circulation in the Indian Ocean as well as in the Mediterranean trade. Archeological research is documenting substantial internal movement of peoples--and with them languages, culture, and technologies--both north-south and east-west within the continent. Commercial links between Africa and the outside world date to the beginning of antiquity.

3. The Kingdom of Kush: The climax of the Meroitic culture occurred from about 250 B.C.E. to 100 C.E. This was an era of prosperity when many monuments were built including royal pyramids, fine pottery and sophisticated iron work. The political system remained stable over many centuries, although royal succession was not from father to son, but within the royal family. Indeed, succession was often determined through the maternal rather than paternal line. We know little of Meroitic administration, yet the sovereign appears to have possessed autocratic power and a bureaucracy that was headed by royal officials; the various provinces were delegated to princes who ruled with considerable autonomy. Slavery existed in Kushite society and their religious worship closely followed Egyptian traditions.

4. Africa to ca. 1000 C.E. in World Perspective: Africa has had important contact and made contributions to other cultures, among them the Hellenistic World, and the Muslim and early Christian societies in northern Africa. For example, St. Augustine of Hippo was an African and Christian monasticism began in Egypt. Africa was engaged with neighbors in trading, in conflict and cooperation, in religious life, and in cultural life. The birth and cultivation of Islam in Africa would affect, redefine, or even eliminate the presence of many previous centers of civilization.

IDENTIFICATION TERMS

For each of the following tell who or what it is, about when did it happen, and why it is significant in the history of the period:

civilization (p. 177):

oral traditions (p. 178):

Nubia (p. 185):

Ethiopia (p. 189):

Nok people (p. 184):

Aksum (p. 189):

Meroe (p. 186):

Napata (p. 185):

tse-tse fly (p. 191):

Bantu (p. 195):

Kush (p. 185):

ivory (p. 197):

"Candaces" (p. 188)

Christian Ethiopia (p. 191):

Khoisan peoples (p. 194):

MULTIPLE CHOICE QUESTIONS

1. Where in Africa is the region of Nubia?
   a. just south of Egypt
   b. south of the equator near the Kalahari Desert
   c. on the west coast of Africa
   d. on the Congo River in central Africa

2. In most of Africa, which of the following poses a perennial problem?
   a. water shortage
   b. lack of abundant animal life
   c. crop pests
   d. both a and c

3. Theories that have linked racial differences to the development and spread of languages, agriculture and state building in Africa
   a. are valid and are becoming generally accepted
   b. are untenable
   c. have revealed new directions toward a progressive study of Africa
   d. both a and c

4. What was the result of the rapid desiccation of the Saharan region in the second millennium B.C.E.?
   a. population dispersal to the eastern Sahara
   b. population dispersal to the Sudanic regions
   c. invasion of the region by conquerors from the East
   d. the transition to bronze tools and weapons

5. By the tenth century B.C.E., Kush
   a. had conquered the Egyptian empire
   b. had emerged as a virtually independent kingdom
   c. had declined and was conquered by the Seleucids
   d. was attacked and conquered by the Egyptians

6. Which of the following represents the correct chronological order of empires in Nilotic Africa and the Ethiopian highlands?
   a. Meroitic empire, Napatan empire, Aksumite empire
   b. Napatan empire, Meroitic empire, Aksumite empire
   c. Aksumite empire, Meroitic empire, Napatan empire
   d. Napatan empire, Aksumite empire, Meroitic empire

7. In the 6th century B.C.E., which of the following had become the center of a flourishing iron industry?
   a. Napata   c. Meroe
   b. Aksum   d. Jenne

8. In the Meroitic empire, political succession
    a. was hereditary from father to son
    b. was often through the maternal rather than paternal line
    c. forbade the possibility of a woman monarch
    d. both a and c

9. The weakened Kushite empire was supplanted about 330 C.E. by
    a. Aksum   c. Nok
    b. Napata   d. Yemen

10. The Aksumite empire was controlled by
    a. a strong priestly class with ties to the eastern Orthodox church
    b. a king of kings through tribute-paying vassals
    c. a commercial oligarchy
    d. a ruling council with limited war making powers

11. The two groups that collectively constitute the Khoisan speakers are the
    a. San and Bantu   c. Khoikhoi and Bantu
    b. San and Khoikhoi   d. Hottentots and Botswanans

12. In the African subcontinent, the vast majority of the peoples speak languages that belong to a single language group known as
    a. Khoisan   c. *Periplus*
    b. Malagasy   d. Bantu

13. Overseas trade with East Africa
    a. was more international than the earliest sources indicate
    b. was minimal at best
    c. extended north to Spain and France
    d. both a and c

14. The most important export from East Africa was
    a. slaves   c. ivory
    b. gold   d. spices

15. From a world perspective, Africa was
    a. engaged with overseas neighbors in extensive trading
    b. important because it was the home of Islam
    c. probably the location where the human species originated
    d. all of the above

STUDY QUESTIONS

1. How would you describe the African continent from a physical perspective? What are the most important rivers, deserts, and climate zones? How has its physical geography, including mineral wealth, soil, water supply, and other natural factors affected the development of societies in Africa?

2. What are some of the problems with racial theories that have attempted to link differences of color or racial type to the development and spread of language, agriculture, iron working, or state building in Africa? Why does the textbook call these theories "untenable?"

3. What were some of the results of the desiccation of the Sahara region after 2500 B.C.E.? What effect did this process have on the distribution of peoples, pottery, and agriculture techniques?

4. Who were the Nok people and why are they important in the study of the early Iron Age in Africa?

5. Discuss the transfer of power from the Napatan empire to the Meroitic empire. What are the specific reasons for the Napatan fall and why was Meroitic Kush able to succeed. In the same manner, discuss the fall of the Meroitic empire and the rise of Aksum. What general statements about the causes of political transition can you make after this analysis?

6. How did the existence of the tse-tse fly affect the development of societies in the western and central Sudan? What role does the transmission of disease have in changing the history of a civilization? Can you think of any other examples from the history of Europe, Asia, or the Americas?

DOCUMENT QUESTIONS

1)   *Herodotus on Carthaginian Trade and on the City of Meroe (p. 187):*

Herodotus was a Greek traveller and historian of the fifth century B.C.E. What can we infer from his description about trade and the interregional contacts of the fifth century B.C.E.?

2)   *A Sixth-century Account of Aksumite Trade (p. 190):*

After reading this passage, what might you infer about the contact of northern East Africa with Arabia and beyond during ancient times?

3)   *Prehistoric Saharan Contact with the Sudan (p. 183):*

Study the picture of the horse drawn chariot on page 183 of your textbook. What does this picture indicate about African trade and why is it important?

4)   *Timbuktu and the Caravan Routes (p. 194):*

Study the photograph of the camel caravan and discuss why the Saharan trade was so dependent on the camel. Would Timbuktu have been able to flourish as a trade center without these "ships of the desert?"

MAP ANALYSIS

Map 6-2: Africa: Early Trade Routes and Early States of the Western and Central Sudan

Study map 6-2 on page 192 of your textbook. Identify the most important trading centers. Why did you make your particular selections? What does this map tell you about the trading activity of the Western and Central Sudan?

MAP EXERCISE

Map 6-1: Africa: Physical Features and Early Sites

Africa is huge and composes one-fifth of the Earth's entire land mass. Its size and diverse physical features often make it difficult for students to comprehend. Look carefully at map 6-1 on page 179 of the textbook and note the main physical features of mountains, savannas, deserts and rivers. Also familiarize yourself with the names of regions and cultures that form the basis of this chapter. Of primary importance are the following: Egypt, Nubia, Kush, Eastern, Western and Central Sudan, Jox (Nok Culture), and Jenne. This map notes the several major regions that are of importance in this chapter: North Africa, Nilotic Africa, the Sudan, West Africa, East Africa, central Africa, and southern Africa. The entire chapter will make a good deal more sense if you spend a bit of time getting yourself oriented geographically. Identify the following sites and physical features of ancient Africa on map 8-1 reproduced on the next page:

1. Western Sudan	7. Egypt
2. Central Sudan	8. Nubia
3. Eastern Sudan	9. Abyssinia
4. Jos plateau	10. Indian Ocean
5. Jenne	11. Kalahari Desert
6. Kush	12. Lake Victoria

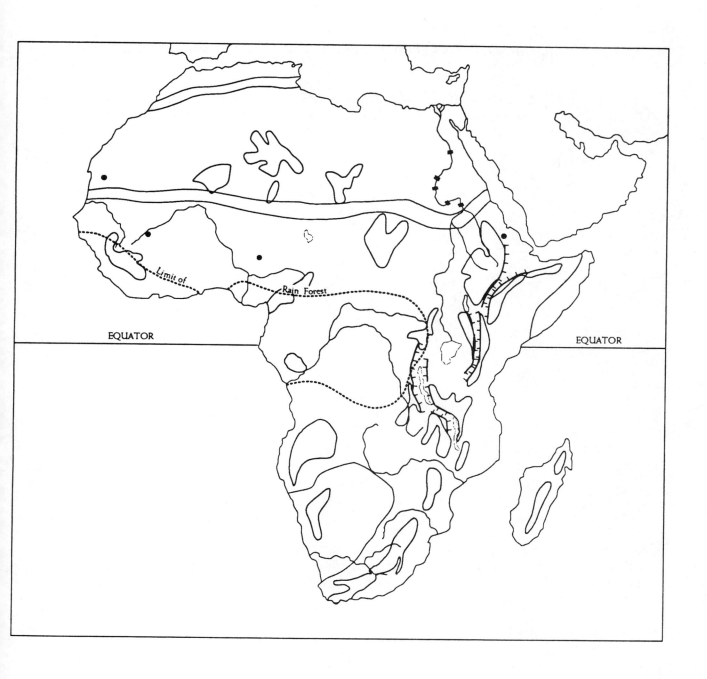

EQUATOR

EQUATOR

Limit of

Rain Forest

MAP 6-1
Africa: Physical Features and Early Sites

Africa: Early History to 1000 C.E.

MULTIPLE CHOICE ANSWER KEY *(with page references)*

1. A (178)	6. B (189)	11. B (195)
2. D (178)	7. C (186)	12. D (195)
3. B (182)	8. B (188)	13. A (197)
4. B (183)	9. A (189)	14. C (197)
5. B (185)	10. B (190)	15. D (198)

China's First Empire (221 B.C.E. - 220 C.E.)

COMMENTARY

This chapter stresses continuity, language and geography in the development of Chinese empires. One of the key turning points in Chinese history was the third century B.C.E., when the old, quasi-feudal Chou multi-state system gave way to a centralized bureaucratic government that built an empire from the steppe in the north to Vietnam in the south. This first empire was divided into three parts: Ch'in dynasty (256-206 B.C.E.), Former Han dynasty (206 B.C.E.- 8 C.E.), and the Later Han dynasty (24-220 C.E.).

The Ch'in dynasty established its control on the geopolitical advantages offered by the Wei River in northwest China. This state was brutal and tough, yet stable. Despite its harsh laws, it attracted farmers who welcomed the security and order of its society. It relied on Legalist Administrators who developed policies for enriching the country and strengthening the military. Under the control of the emperor, the Ch'in dynasty expanded its territorial holdings, instituted bureaucratic reforms and stressed uniformity of thought in establishing a centralized state. The Great Wall of China was extended some fourteen hundred miles from the Pacific Ocean to central Asia and is testament to the efficiency and control of this dynasty. However, too many changes in rapid succession caused the entire system to collapse under the harsh rule of the dynasty. Rebellion spread as the Ch'in government lost its popular support.

The first emperor of the Han dynasty, Kao Tsu of plebeian origin, established the capital in the Wei basin close to the former capitals of the Chou and Ch'in dynasties. Although it took many years to consolidate power, this action permitted a degree of continuity to exist in the political development of China. The second phase of the dynastic cycle began with the rule of the "martial emperor," Wu Ti, in 141 B.C.E. Old policies like government monopolies on salt, iron, liquor, etc. were established to maintain control of China. Wu Ti expanded the boundaries of China by sweeping south into North Vietnam and north to central Manchuria and North Korea. This aggressive leadership created a strong army and led to the policy of "using the barbarians to control the barbarians," thus making allies of border nomads against those more distant. This policy worked for the most part and brought about the establishment of the Silk Road that connected with the Roman Empire.

During the course of the Han dynasty, the Legalist structure of government became partially Confucianized. The Confucian classics gradually were accepted as the standard for education and served as an ethical justification for dynastic rule. After a period of instability and civil war in which contending factions tried to establish hegemony, the Han dynasty was restored and ruled from 25-220 C.E. This "Later Han" period saw a return to strong central government and a laissez-faire economy. Their armies crossed the Gobi desert and defeated the northern Hsiung Nu who migrated to the west where they were known during the 5th century C.E. as the Huns of Attila. Until 88 C.E., the emperors of the Later Han were vigorous, but afterward they were ineffective and short-lived. Political instability caused by plotting empresses, eunuch conspiracies and religious rebellion plagued the dynasty until it was overthrown by the military in 220 C.E. For more than three and a half centuries after the fall of the Han, China was disunited and dominated by aristocratic landowning families. During this period, north and south China developed in different ways. In the south, a succession of six short-lived dynasties centered themselves around the capital of Nanking and prospered economically, although political chaos was the order of the day. In the north, state formation resulted from the interaction of nomadic tribes with the Chinese population. The short-lived states that were organized are usually referred to as the Sixteen Kingdoms. Amid endemic wars and differences in languages, Buddhism was a common denominator and served as a bridge between "barbarians" and Chinese.

The Han period was creative in many ways, but excelled in philosophy and history. Many Confucian texts were recovered during this time and scholars began writing commentaries on the classics. The Chinese were the greatest historians of the premodern world and emphasized primary source evaluation. As the Han would in influence, some scholars abandoned Confucianism altogether in favor of Neo-Taoism or "mysterious learning;" this was a reaction against the rigidity of Confucian doctrine and defined the natural as pleasurable. They sought immortality in dietary restrictions, meditation, sexual abstinence or orgies, and emphasized an amalgam of beliefs including an afterlife of innumerable heavens and hells where good and evil would be recompensed. The text goes on to discuss Buddhist doctrine and its spread into China. As the socio-political order collapsed in the third century C.E., Buddhism spread rapidly and was especially influential by the fifth century.

KEY POINTS AND VITAL CONCEPTS

1. The Dynastic Cycle: Historians of China have seen a pattern in every dynasty of long duration. This dynastic cycle begins with internal wars that eventually lead to the military unification of China. The successful unifier then justifies his rule by emphasizing that he has a mandate from heaven. The emperor consolidates his power, restores peace and order to China and launches several energetic reforms and public works projects. During the peak of this phase, China expands militarily and appears invincible. But then the cycle turns downward because of the increased costs of empire and opulence at court, which require additional taxes on a burdened populace. The vigor of the monarch wanes, intrigues develop and central controls loosen as provincial governors and military commanders gain autonomy. Finally, public works fall into disrepair, rebellions break out and the dynasty collapses. In the view of Confucian historians, the last emperors were not only politically weak, but morally culpable as well.

2. Contenders for Imperial Power: The court during the Han dynasty exhibited features that would appear in later dynasties as well. The emperor was the "Son of Heaven," omniscient and omnipotent in his authority. Yet when he was weak or a child, others ruled in his name and they emerged from four distinct categories: 1) officials who staffed the apparatus of government 2) the empress dowager whose child had been named heir to the throne 3) court eunuchs who served in the emperor's harem and often cultivated influence as confidants, and 4) military commanders who became semi-independent rulers and occasionally even usurped the position of the emperor in the later phases of dynastic rule. Yet they were less powerful than commanders in the Roman Empire because their authority was limited to a single campaign and commanders were appointed in pairs so each would check the other.

3. The Spread of Buddhism: Central Asian missionaries brought Buddhism to China in the first century where it was first recognized as a new Taoist sect. As the Han socio-political order collapsed in the third century C.E., Buddhism spread rapidly until it was firmly entrenched by the fifth century. Though an alien religion in China, Buddhism had some advantages over Taoism: 1) It was a doctrine of personal salvation 2) It contained high standards of personal ethics 3) It continued to receive inspiration from the sophisticated meditative practices of the Indian tradition. The core of Buddhist teaching is the realization of simple truths: Life is suffering, the cause of suffering is desire; death does not end the endless cycle of birth and rebirth; only the attainment of nirvana releases one from the "wheel of Karma." Thus all of the cosmic drama of salvation is centered in the figure of Buddha.

4. China's First Empire in World Context: The great empires in China, India and the Mediterranean all came after revolutions in thought where the conception of universal political authority derived from earlier philosophies. All three empires joined their Iron Age technologies with new organizational techniques to create superb military forces. Yet there were differences as well: 1) China was a much more homogeneous culture than was the polyglot empire of Rome 2) government in Han China was more orderly, complex and competent. Government officials controlled the military almost until the end, whereas Rome suffered from chaotic leadership in the third century C.E. and was in no sense a dynasty 3) Roman power and unity was built gradually over centuries, whereas China remained a multi-state system right up to 232 B.C.E. and then was unified by one state in eleven years.

IDENTIFICATION TERMS

For each of the following, tell who or what it is, about when did it happen, and why it is significant in the history of the period:

Wu Ti (p. 205):

"Salt and Iron Debate" (p. 205):

Great Wall (p. 203):

Prefectures (p. 202):

Journey to the West (p. 214):

"Son of Heaven" (p. 206):

Dynastic cycle (p. 204):

Hsiung Nu (p. 208):

Kao Tsu (p. 205):

"First emperor" (p. 202):

Neo-Taoism (p. 213):

"Wheel of Karma" (p. 215):

Wang Mang (p. 208):

Tales of the Three Kingdoms (p. 209):

Li Ssu (p. 202):

MULTIPLE CHOICE QUESTIONS

1. China was unified by the
   - a. Ch'in dynasty
   - b. Former Han dynasty
   - c. Later Han dynasty
   - d. Chou dynasty

2. The Ch'in state was located on the
   - a. Yellow River
   - b. Huai River
   - c. Wei River
   - d. Yangtze River

3. The Great Wall of China was built to
   - a. consolidate the diverse peoples under Ch'in rule
   - b. protect against the incursion of aggressive tribes from the north
   - c. split the Ch'in and Chou kingdoms
   - d. establish clear boundaries between prefectures

4. After the death of the First Emperor in 210 B.C.E., the Ch'in dynasty
   - a. was destroyed by the domino effect of its own legal codes
   - b. maintained its organization under the rule of Wang Mang
   - c. was destroyed under pressure by the Yellow Turbans
   - d. both a and c

5. The "dynastic cycle" begins with
   - a. internal wars
   - b. economic growth
   - c. strong centralized political authority
   - d. both b and c

6. In the "Salt and Iron Debate," Confucian scholars argued that
   - a. the state should enjoy the profits from the sale of salt and iron
   - b. salt and iron should be left in private ownership
   - c. the government should expand their territory in search of resources
   - d. Japan should be allowed to join the search for resources in China

7. The Former Han dynasty
   - a. reduced the centralized bureaucracy
   - b. relied on a Legalist administrative structure
   - c. continued the centralized bureaucratic administration of the Ch'in
   - d. both b and c

8. The "son of heaven" was a title that provided
    a. justification for republican rule
    b. complete power for the empress dowager
    c. an ethical justification for dynastic rule
    d. none of the above

9. The pilgrimage of the Tang monk, Hsuan Tsang, was novelized as
    a. *Journey to Karma*   c. *Journey to the West*
    b. *The Yellow Turban*   d. *The Red Eyebrows*

10. On the death of the emperor Kao Tsu in 195 B.C.E., China was
    a. overrun by the Hsiung Nu
    b. controlled by the Empress Lu
    c. ruled by Wang Mang
    d. none of the above

11. In the teachings of Confucius, a woman obeyed her
    a. parents   c. son
    b. husband   d. all of the above

12. *Tales of the Three Kingdoms* was a
    a. compilation of military stories
    b. nationalistic piece of propaganda
    c. Confucian history
    d. great romantic epic of Chinese literature

13. Han philosophy
    a. has been criticized for having a mechanistic view of nature
    b. tries to encompass the interrelationships of the natural world
    c. spurred advances in astronomy, music, and medicine
    d. all of the above

14. Ssu-Ma Ch'ien was famous for his
    a. Neo-Taoist philosophy   c. *Spring and Autumn Annals*
    b. history of the known world   d. both b and c

15. Which of the following was an advantage that Buddhism had over Taoism in the competition between
    the two religions:
    a. Buddhism offered no concept of an afterlife
    b. Buddhism contained high standards of personal ethics
    c. Buddhism rejected the complex Indian tradition of meditative practices
    d. Buddhism was never persecuted

STUDY QUESTIONS

1.   What were the major reasons for the success of the expansion of the Ch'in empire? What were the geographic limits of the empire? Why was the Great Wall built and to what extent did it achieve its major purpose? How did the bureaucracy function?

2.   How did the Former Han rulers continue the policies of the Ch'in dynasty? How were they different?   Why did the Silk Road come into existence in this time period?

3.   What was the <u>dynastic cycle</u> in China? Why was there a specific mandate from heaven for this political activity?   What were the general reasons for a downward trend in the cycle?

4.   After the collapse of the Later Han dynasty, why did the south prosper with the capital at Nanking? What factors were important in developing a sound economy and attracting Chinese to the south? What role did religion play in this development?

5.   What were the contributions of philosophy to the Han dynasty? How did philosophy aid in uniting the large empire? What were some of the major controversies of the time?

6.   Why did Buddhism appeal to the Chinese? Why were some of the Indian practices utilized by many who became involved in the faith? What importance did the collapse of the Han dynasty have in this movement?

DOCUMENT QUESTIONS

1)   *The Position of Women (p. 209):*

   What general image of the social position of women during the Han Dynasty can you glean from this source? What specific lines of this poem are particularly revealing?

2)   *Ssu-ma Ch'ien on the Wealthy (p. 212):*

   What does this source tell you about the economic life of Han cities? What does Ssu-ma Ch'ien think about the aristocracy? What does this tell you about Chinese society during this time period?

3)   *Chinese Women Among the Nomads (p. 207):*

Compare this source with that on page 209 about the lot of women in Chinese society. What does the fate of the women suggest about the foreign policy of the rulers of ancient China?

4)   *Peach Blossom Spring (p. 214):*

Why is this story so appealing? Why is the ending especially poignant? What values in life are most important to Ta'o Ch'ien?

MAP ANALYSIS

Map 7-1: The Unification of China by the Ch'in State (221-206 B.C.E.)

Study Map 7-1 on page 202 of the textbook. How impressive was the Ch'in accomplishment of unification? Look at the picture of the Great Wall on page 203 and note it's length on the map. Why was it constructed and how was it essential to the unification program?

MULTIPLE CHOICE ANSWER KEY *(with page references)*

1. A (202)	6. B (205)	11. D (209)
2. C (202)	7. D (205)	12. D (209)
3. B (202)	8. C (206)	13. D (211)
4. A (203)	9. C (214)	14. B (213)
5. A (204)	10. B (206)	15. B (213)

Imperial China (589-1368)

COMMENTARY

This chapter concentrates on China's imperial age and emphasizes the cultural and philosophical contributions of this important period. During this time, which corresponds to the European "middle ages," the most notable feature of Chinese history was the reunification of China and the recreation of a centralized bureaucratic empire consciously modeled on the earlier Han dynasty (206 B.C.E.-220 C.E.). China was able to develop a unified state at a time when political fragmentation in Europe brought about small, independent kingdoms.

The Sui dynasty (589-618) sprang from Chinese-Turkish origins, reestablished a centralized bureaucracy and rebuilt the Great Wall and other public works. After a period of political disintegration and civil war among contending aristocratic factions, the T'ang dynasty was established. Chinese historians have often compared the short-lived Sui dynasty with that of the Ch'in in that it provided a foundation for the subsequent progress of China.

The T'ang dynasty (618-907) established an efficient bureaucracy through frugality, and expanded Chinese borders to their greatest extent. The chapter explains the intricacies of T'ang administration especially during the years of good rule from 624-755. Although the government was centered around the figure of the emperor, aristocrats were given generous tax concessions and served as officials at court. Women continued to play a role in government; a concubine, Wu Chao, (625-706) ruled for seven years as regent before she deposed her son and ascended to sole power herself.

The reign of the emperor Hsuan-Tsung (713-756) is particularly noted for its cultural brilliance and the capital grew to approximately 2 million people. The T'ang dynasty applied a four tier foreign policy of military aggression, use of nomads against other nomadic tribes, establishment of strong border defenses (Great Wall), and diplomatic action. However, during the mid-eighth century, China's frontiers began to contract and external enemies in Manchuria and Tibet contributed to growing internal dissension. By 907, the T'ang dynasty had been carried into independent kingdoms. Still, the fall of the T'ang did not lead to the kind of division that had followed the Han.

The chapter continues with a section on T'ang culture. The creativity of the T'ang period arose from the juxtaposition and interaction of cosmopolitan, medieval Buddhist and secular elements. T'ang culture was cosmopolitan not just because of its broad contacts with other cultures and peoples, but because of its openness to them.

The reestablishment of a centralized bureaucracy stimulated the tradition of learning and contributed to the reappearance of secular scholarship. For the first time, scholars wrote comprehensive institutional histories, compiled dictionaries, and wrote commentaries on the Confucian classics. The most famous poets of the period were Li Po (701-762) and Tu Fu (712-770), who were often quite secular in their literary approach.

The Sung dynasty (960-1279) continued the normal pattern of dynastic cycles set in Chinese history. The breakdown of the empire into northern and southern sections after 1127 was followed by the Mongol conquest of the Southern Sung in 1279. Instead of a detailed enumeration of emperors and court officials, the chapter emphasizes the various changes during the T'ang and Sung dynasties that affected China's agriculture, society, economy, state and culture; taken together, the developments in these areas explain why China did not lapse into disunity after the political collapse of the T'ang dynasty.

The greatest achievements of the Sung dynasty were in philosophy, poetry and painting. The chapter details the Neo-Confucian ideas of Chu Hsi (1130-1200), which brought a degree of stability to Chinese society. The outstanding poet of the period was Su Tung Po (1037-1101), who believed in a limited role for government and social control through morality. A leading painting style was created by Shih K'o in which human figures were not the dominant focus of the art form.

The Sung dynasty collapsed by 1279, under the military dominance of the Mongols. Genghis Khan united the various Mongol tribes and, bent on world domination, established an empire that extended from the Caspian Sea to the Pacific Ocean. The Mongol rule in China is but a chapter of a larger story. In 1279, under Genghis' grandson, Kublai, the Yuan dynasty was established, but did not change Chinese high culture to any degree. The language barrier assisted in preserving the Chinese way of life. The Southern Sung area was the last to be conquered and the least altered by Mongol control. The Yuan dynasty collapsed in 1368.

KEY POINTS AND VITAL CONCEPTS

1. <u>Varieties of Buddhism</u>: During the early T'ang, the principal Buddhist sect was the T'ien-t'ai. But because of its 9th century suppression, other sects came to the fore. They included Maitreya (Mi Lo), a Buddha of the future who will appear and create a paradise on earth; Amitabha (A Mi T'o), the Lord of the Western Paradise, who helped humans obtain salvation and whose sect was the largest in China; and finally, Ch'an, or Zen in Japanese. Zen was anti-intellectual in its emphasis on direct intuition into one's own Buddha-nature. It taught that the historical Buddha was only a man and exhorted each person to attain enlightenment by his or her own efforts. The discipline of meditation, combined with a Zen view of nature profoundly influenced the arts in China, Korea and Japan.

2. <u>Mongol Control of China</u>: The Mongol's major objective in the world was to conquer China. This movement brought them into contact with other superior civilizations. However, the major concentration on China diverted their small resource base to lessen the impact on the Chinese population. Therefore, the high culture of China was not lost to the barbarians and after the fall of the Yuan dynasty in 1368, Chinese civilization continued in the pattern of the great empires. The Mongol efficiency in controlling empire proved to be a greater obstacle than the more populated areas could overcome. The four groups, with the Mongols at the top and the Chinese at the bottom, brought about division within the Yuan Empire. The continued language barrier between the Mongols, speaking Altaic, and the Chinese brought constant friction to the area. This activity did not permit the Chinese civilization to continue in a manner much the same as before the arrival of the Mongols.

3. <u>Imperial China in World Perspective</u>: Rough parallels between China and Europe persisted until the 6th century C.E. But then, a fundamental divergence occurred. Europe tailed off into centuries of feudal disunity while China reunited and attained a new level of wealth, power and culture. Why? One reason was that the victory of Buddhism was less complete than that of Christianity in Europe. Confucianism survived within aristocratic families and the concept of a united empire was integral to it. In contrast, the Roman conception of political order was not maintained as an independent doctrine, and empire was not a vital concept in western Christian thought. In addition, China possessed a greater cultural homogeneity and higher population density; this explains why China could absorb barbarian conquerors more quickly than could Europe. Although comparisons across continents are difficult, it seems likely that T'ang and Sung China had longer stretches of good government than any other part of their contemporary world. Not until the nineteenth century would comparable bureaucracies of talent and virtue begin to appear in the West.

Imperial China (589 - 1368)

IDENTIFICATION TERMS

For each of the following, tell who or what it is, about when did it happen, and why it is significant in the history of the period:

Circuit (p. 250):

Tu Fu (p. 236):

Kublai Khan (p. 245):

A Description of the World (p. 247):

Sui Wen-ti (p. 228):

Caves of the Thousand Buddhas (p. 234):

equal field system (p. 229):

Mi Lo (p. 235):

Empress Wu Chao (p. 229):

Chu Hsi (p. 241):

"Great Ultimate" (p. 241):

Su Tung-P'o (p. 242):

Li Po (p. 235):

Shamans (p. 244):

Zen (p. 235):

MULTIPLE CHOICE QUESTIONS

1. The most notable feature of Chinese history during the Sui and T'ang dynasties was the
    a. reunification of China
    b. disintegration of emperor worship
    c. recreation of a centralized bureaucratic empire
    d. both a and c

2. The throne in the Northern Wei was insecure and often usurped because the
    a. military was controlled by professional generals
    b. social distance between aristocracy and royalty was small
    c. state had no firm geographical barriers
    d. all of the above

3. During the reign of Sui Wen-ti, the Sui dynasty
    a. rebuilt the Great Wall
    b. built huge palaces
    c. restored the tax base
    d. all of the above

4. The Sui dynasty declined because
    a. the court became corrupt and demoralized
    b. aggressive tribes invaded from Japan
    c. the loss of Chinese lives in wars with Korea produced discontent
    d. both a and c

5. The most important body in the T'ang administration was the
    a. Council of State
    b. Secretariat
    c. Censorate
    d. Chancellery

6. The "equal field system"
    a. was part of the Sui tax system
    b. was egalitarian for all able-bodied men
    c. gave special exemptions and advantages to the aristocracy
    d. both a and c

7. The Empress Wu Chao
    a. was a patron of the arts
    b. advocated state subsidies for poets
    c. murdered or exiled her rivals at court
    d. all of the above

8. After the Empress Wu Chao,
    a. the T'ang dynasty fell into political chaos
    b. no woman would ever become emperor again
    c. the Scholars of the North Gate were exiled
    d. the old northeastern Chinese aristocrats were exiled

9. The principal threats to the T'ang state were the
   a. Tibetans   c. Khitan Mongols
   b. Turks   d. all of the above

10. In their foreign relations, the T'ang dynasty
   a. refused to make allies
   b. generally conquered as many neighbors as possible
   c. employed a four-tier policy of defenses
   d. relied on the protection of Japan

11. Among the most important of achievements during the T'ang dynasty was the
   a. reform of the land system
   b. development of commercial contacts with neighboring countries
   c. consolidation of autonomous provinces
   d. destruction of renegade warlords

12. Which dynasty was associated with the Golden Age of Buddhism in China?
   a. Sui   c. Sung
   b. T'ang   d. Yuan

13. The millennium of late imperial China after the T'ang is often spoken of as the
   a. Age of Autocracy   c. Age of Imperialism
   b. Age of Absolute Monarchy   d. both a and b

14. The Sung culture differed from that of the T'ang in that it became more
   a. intensely and narrowly Chinese
   b. expansive and inclusive of Japanese culture
   c. eclectic in nature
   d. none of the above

15. The greatest of Mongol leaders was
   a. Chang Chi-chih   c. Chu Hsi
   b. Genghis Kahn   d. Su Tung-p'o

STUDY QUESTIONS

1. What is the importance of the Sui dynasty to the T'ang dynasty? What former Chinese empire developed a role model for these two dynasties? What great building program developed in the Sui period?

2. Why was Empress Wu (625-706) successful in obtaining control in the T'ang period? How did her role affect Chinese history? Did her influence enhance or detract from the prestige of the T'ang empire?

3. Describe how peasants in China changed from serfs to free farmers. What was the role of the aristocracy in this transformation? Why did the equal field system collapse?

4. Discuss the influence of technological changes during the Sung period. What was the impact of money on trade? Why did the population shift to the south? What role did the scholar-gentry play in these changes?

5. Describe the methods utilized by the Mongols to control China. What advantage was there in maintaining a language barrier between the Mongols and the Chinese? How did the "myriad system" work?

6. Discuss the major differences between Europe and China after 500. What was the importance of Buddhism in China? What role did the mandate from heaven have in the Chinese concept of empire? Why and how did language and population influence the Chinese development?

DOCUMENT QUESTIONS

1)   T'ang Government Organization (p. 230):

The textbook notes that the emperor wanted a bureaucratic government in which "authority was centralized in his own person. On the other hand, he had to make concessions to the aristocrats...who staffed his government." After studying this chart, how successful was the emperor in achieving a personal rule without neglecting his aristocracy? How were the aristocracy used in the government?

2)   A Clerk Thinks About His Career (p. 240):

What is the main complaint of this clerk about his situation? Why can't he get ahead? What does he mean by "Everything, I guess, is a matter of Fate"? What does his lament tell you about the quality of bureaucrats in the T'ang government?

3) *Poems by Li Po (p. 237):*

What does this lament by a river merchant's wife tell you about the expectation of women in China during this period? Compare this with the photograph of the pottery figures on page 230. Does it strike you odd that court ladies should be playing polo on horseback? What does this tell you about how women were viewed during the T'ang dynasty?

4) *Marco Polo Describes the City of Hangchow (p. 248):*

Who was Marco Polo and why was he in China during the 13th century C.E.? What was his view of Chinese society according to this account about Hangchow? What seems to impress Marco Polo the most?

MAP ANALYSIS

Map 8-3: The Mongol Empire in the Late Thirteenth Century

Study this map carefully on page 246 of your textbook. How was this extensive empire organized? What were the boundaries of the Mongol empire? Note especially the Mongol invasion attempts--why do you think that these failed when the Mongols had such success elsewhere?

MAP EXERCISE

Map 8-1: The T'ang Empire at its Peak During the Eighth Century

The T'ang Empire reached its peak in the eighth century. Study Map 8-1 on page 229 of your textbook. On the map provided on the next page of this *Study Guide*, shade in the area of the T'ang Empire and identify the following:

1. Ch'ang-an

2. Loyang

3. Yangtze River

4. Yellow River

5. Tibet

6. Japan

7. Nomadic Turkic Peoples

8. Tarim Basin

9. Silla

10. Kunlun Mountains

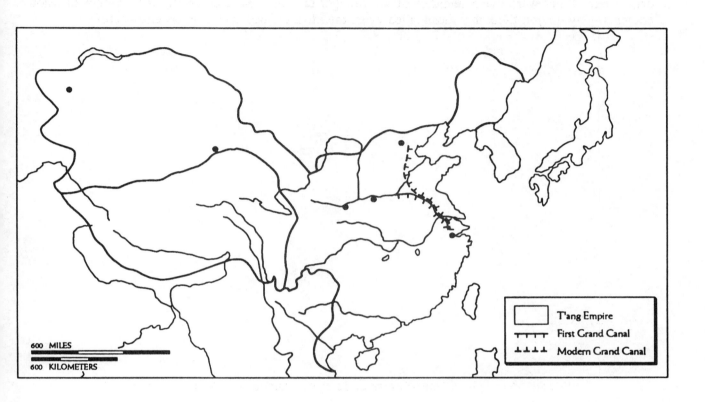

MAP 8-1
T'ang Empire at its Peak During the Eighth Century

MULTIPLE CHOICE ANSWER KEY *(with page references)*

1. D (227)	6. C (229)	11. A (233)
2. B (227)	7. C (229)	12. B (234)
3. D (228)	8. B (230)	13. D (239)
4. D (228)	9. D (231)	14. A (241)
5. A (229)	10. C (231)	15. B (244)

9

Japan: Early History to 1467

COMMENTARY

The chapter emphasizes the importance of the T'ang dynasty of China in spreading civilization to Japan, Vietnam and Korea. Japanese historic development began with the Jomon culture and was replaced about 300 B.C.E. by immigrants from the Korean peninsula who established the Yayoi culture. They contributed their expertise in using bronze and iron. Emerging directly from the Yayoi culture was a period from 300-600 C.E. characterized by tomb mounds. The Yamato period is known to us through Chinese records and the earliest Japanese accounts of its own history: *Records of Ancient Matters and Records of Japan*. They recall political power struggles at court between aristocratic families and constant wars in outlying regions. The Yamato period continued to be influenced by Koreans who introduced Buddhism to Japan in 532. The indigenous religion of Japan, however, was an animistic worship of the forces of nature called *Shinto* or "the way of the gods."

A major turning point in Japanese history was its adoption of the higher civilization of China beginning in the early seventh century. The emperor Temmu (673-686) established a kingship along Chinese lines, styling himself as the "heavenly emperor." The emperors at the Nara (710-794) and Heian (794-1156) courts in Japan were both Confucian rulers with the majesty accorded by Chinese law, and Shinto rulers descended from the Sun Goddess. Protected by an aura of the sacred, their lineage was never usurped; all Japanese history constitutes a single dynasty. The chapter then details the Japanese governmental structure, noting the similarities and differences with that of China.

The conscript armies of the Nara had proved ineffective so the courts abolished conscription and began a new system based on local mounted warriors called samurai ("those who serve"). Their primary weapon was the bow and arrow, used from the saddle. The samurai generally came from well-to-do local families who could afford to supply the costly weapons. Their initial function was to preserve local order and help with tax collection. But they also contributed to disorder as regional military coalitions formed from the tenth century. The chapter goes on to detail governmental institutions and administrative relationships during the late-Heian period. Power was often shared between emperors and noble clans such as the Fujiwara. In 1156, the House of Taira assumed control of Japan through support of a military coalition.

The culture in Heian Japan was quickly assimilated from the T'ang culture of China and was the exclusive preserve of the aristocracy. This explains why aristocrats found commoners to be odd and hardly human. The Chinese tradition remained strong and most writing of the period, including legal codes, was done in Chinese. Japanese writing developed in the ninth century with the introduction of the *Kana*, a syllabic script or alphabet. The greatest works of the period were the *Pillow Book* and the first novel, *Tales of Genji*, both written by women around 1010. These literary tracts reflect wit, sensitivity and psychological delineation of character.

In Japan, Buddhism grew gradually during the seventh and eighth centuries. The Japanese came to Buddhism not from the philosophical perspectives of Confucianism or Taoism, but from the magic and mystery of Shinto. The appeal of Buddhism to the early Japanese was in its colorful and elaborate rituals. Two new Buddhist sects, the Tendai and Shingon, were established respectively by Saicho and Kukai in the late eighth and early ninth centuries. Shinto religion was generally absorbed into the faith and only disentangled from Buddhism in the mid-nineteenth century.

The year 1185 was a major turning point in Japanese history. It began a shift from centuries of rule by a civil aristocracy to centuries of military control. It saw the formation of the *bakufu* (tent government), a completely non-Chinese type of government under the initial leadership of Minamoto Yoritomo. Centering his rule in Kamakura, this bakufu lasted from 1185-1333. This period also saw the emergence of the *shogun* as the *de facto* ruler of Japan, though in theory he was but a military official of the emperor. It marked the beginning of new cultural forms and changes in family and social organization. The chapter details the rule of Yoritomo, Kamakura feudalism and the role of women in a warrior society.

Between 1331 and 1336, Japan entered upon a period of turmoil from which emerged a regional multistate system centering on Kyoto, called the Ashikaga Bakufu (1336-1467). Each region was based on a warrior band, and civil and military posts were fused, which provided a greater degree of control over the population.

The chapter concludes with an assessment of Buddhism and medieval culture. Zen, in particular, influenced the arts of medieval Japan. Aristocratic creativity was often seen as grounded in the experience of meditation. There were new art forms as well such as *No* Play, a kind of mystery drama with no parallels in East Asia.

KEY POINTS AND VITAL CONCEPTS

1. <u>Chinese Influence on Japan</u>: Chinese civilization was a key element in influencing the culture and government of Japan. Official embassies to China began in 607 C.E. and the Japanese who studied there played key roles in their government when they returned. Chinese writings were used in official documents, histories and legal codes. Japanese writing only developed with the Kana in the ninth century. The *No* Play of the Ashikaga period was a unique move away from Chinese influence.

2. *<u>Shogun</u> and <u>Samurai</u>*: By 1200, Japanese military forces had emerged as an organized and potent force for change or stability. The samurai warriors hailed primarily from local aristocracy and gave relative influence to provincial strongmen as a feudal society similar to the European experience developed. The Mongol invasions of 1274 and 1281 brought more power to the hands of the military as the country required protection. Peasants were reduced to serf status and the society was regulated. At first the shogun served as the primary military commander for the emperor, but by 1200, emperors generally remained in a figurehead position.

3. <u>Japanese Chronology</u>: Japanese history has three main turning points, each marked by a major influx of outside culture and each followed by a massive restructuring of Japanese institutions:
   A)   ***Third century B.C.E. - 600 C.E.***:   Old Stone Age Japan became an agricultural metal-working society.
   B)   ***600 - ca. 1850***:   Japan is influenced by Chinese culture and leaps to a higher civilization with the development of a writing system, new technologies and philosophies. This period can be further subdivided as follows:
          710 - 794:   Nara Japan
          794 - 1156:   Heian Japan
   Rule by Military Houses
          1156 - 1180:   Taira rule
          1185 - 1333:   The Kamakura Bakufu (Yoritomo, Hojo, etc.)
          1333 - 1336:   Disputed control
          1336 - 1467:   The Ashikaga Bakufu
   C)   ***Ca. 1850 - Present***:   Japan encounters western civilizations.

4. <u>Early Japanese History in World Perspective</u>: The spread of civilization in East Asia from its heartland in China was more rapid than in the West because the T'ang empire of China had been reestablished on a more vital plane. Vietnam, Korea and Japan all took advantage of the Chinese model. Yet, because of Japan's large population and distance from China, it proved eventually to be a strong variant to the Chinese pattern in East Asian civilization. Both Japan and western Europe had centuries of feudalism and both areas began as backward societies onto which "heartland cultures" were grafted during the first millennium C.E.

IDENTIFICATION TERMS

For each of the following tell who or what it is, about when did it happen, and why it is significant in the history of the period:

Minatomo (p. 266):

Kana (p. 262):

Shinto (p. 256):

Pimiko (p. 254):

Pillow Book (p. 262):

"tomb culture" (p. 254):

bakufu (p. 266):

The Tale of Genji (p. 263):

Yamato Period (p. 255):

Ashikaga (p. 270):

Tendai Buddhism (p. 266):

shogun (p. 266):

Yayoi revolution (p. 254):

Shingon Buddhism (p. 266):

Temmu (p. 258):

MULTIPLE CHOICE QUESTIONS

1. Each of the three main turning points in Japanese history was marked by
    a. the military defeat of Japanese armies
    b. a massive restructuring of Japanese institutions
    c. a major influx of an outside culture
    d. both b and c

2. The second phase of Japanese prehistory began about 300 B.C.E. with the
    a. Yayoi revolution
    b. Yamato state
    c. Jomon culture
    d. Tomb culture of the T'ang

3. During the third century C.E., a temporary hegemony was achieved over Japanese regional tribal confederations by
    a. the Yamato "great kings"
    b. Korean invaders
    c. a queen named Pimiko
    d. the "Paekche connection"

4. The indigenous religion of Yamato Japan was an animistic worship of the forces of nature called
    a. *uji*
    b. *Shinto*
    c. *Kyushu*
    d. *Kamo*

5. Large scale institutional changes in Japanese government began in the 680's under the leadership of the
    a. Emperor Temmu
    b. Emperor Shirakawa
    c. Empress Jito
    d. both a and c

6. The emperors at the Nara and Heian courts were
    a. Confucian rulers
    b. Shinto rulers
    c. considered descendants of the sun goddess
    d. all of the above

7. The *samurai* military system developed after 792 because
    a. conscription had proved to be inefficient
    b. the Mongols invaded and the Japanese nobility were the primary resisters
    c. the government could not afford to pay armies of free soldiers
    d. mercenary forces were often disloyal

8. Fujiwara rule gave way, during the second half of the 11th century to rule by
    a. military governors
    b. retired emperors
    c. specially appointed audit and police commissioners
    d. feuding *samurai* warriors

9. *Kana* was
   a. a syllabic script which was developed during the 9th century
   b. a series of Chinese characters that were used as phonetic symbols
   c. a Japanese concept expressing the idea of "Fate"
   d. none of the above

10. The world's first novel was
    a. *Ten Thousand Leaves*   c. *Collection of Ancient and Modern Times*
    b. *Tale of Genji*   d. *The Pillow Book*

11. The two great Buddhist sects of the Heian era in Japan were
    a. Koya and Kana   c. Yakushiji and Amaro
    b. Sugawara and Michizane   d. Tendai and Shingon

12. The period 1160-1185 marked another major turning point in Japanese history because it
    a. began the shift from centuries of rule by a civil aristocracy to rule by the military
    b. saw the formation of the *bakufu*
    c. saw the emergence of the *shogun* as the de facto ruler of Japan
    d. all of the above

13. The invasion of Japan in 1281 by the Mongols was unsuccessful because
    a. Japanese tactics of fierce individual combat decimated the Mongol army
    b. the Kyoto court captured and beheaded Kublai Khan
    c. *kamikaze* sank a portion of the Mongol fleet
    d. both a and c

14. After the decline of Kamakura hegemony about 1335,
    a. Japan was finally conquered by the Mongols
    b. Ashikaga Takauji established a regional multistate system under the control of vassals
    c. power was transferred to the Nun Shogun
    d. Minamoto Yoritomo established his personal *bakufu*

15. The most remarkable aspect of Zen Buddhism was its
    a. influence on the arts of Japan
    b. emphasis on book learning and the "complex mind"
    c. lack of influence from China
    d. rejection of meditation and emphasis on interaction with the political world

STUDY QUESTIONS

1. What were the major characteristics of earlier religions in Japan? How did Shintoism differ from Buddhism? In what manner was this development different from religions in China? Why was this movement confined to the islands of Japan?

2. What was the agricultural system in use up to 838? Why did the "quota and estate" system come into existence? What was the role of the Samurai in this development?

3. How did the Fujiwara clan rule from 856 to 1056? Why did the retired emperors gain control from this group? What was the importance of Kyoto, as the political center, from 710 to 1180?

4. What were the important cultural contributions of the Nara and Heian periods in Japan? What was the first novel ever written and the impact of this book on the Japanese upper class?

5. Why did the Mongol invasions of Japan fail? Where did the attacks take place? What was the Japanese main defense? What were the domestic political repercussions of these invasions on Japan?

6. How did commerce start in Japan and what products formed the base of trade? How did this activity alter Japanese society? Why did commerce develop at such a late time period compared to China?

DOCUMENT QUESTIONS

1)   *Aristocratic Taste at the Fujiwara Court (p. 264):*

Read the several sections offered in this excerpt from *The Pillow Book* of Sei Shonagon. Which of them do you like the most and why? What do these excerpts say about Japanese society? Why is *The Pillow Book* such a popular piece of literature?

2)   *Mongol Invaders Battle Samurai Horseman (p. 269):*

Analyze this picture and describe the military armaments of the Mongols. Why is one lone *samurai* horseman able to defeat ten Mongols? Does this painting have propaganda value?

3)   *A Sermon by the Pure Land Monk Ippen (p. 272):*

In this painting, note the crowded conditions within a very restricted area for the sermon by Ippen. Why did the aristocrats insist on taking their carriages with them into such a crowded space? What generalizations about Pure Land Buddhism can you make from the fact that commoners and aristocrats could share facilities for the sermon?

4)   *The Arts and Zen Buddhism (p. 276):*

How does this source display the basic principles of Zen Buddhism? How does one link "all the artistic powers with one mind"? To the question, "Where should a swordsman fix his mind"?, how logically does the author arrive at the conclusion, "Thus the mind should not be fixed anywhere"? What does this mean?

MAP ANALYSIS

Map 9-2: Medieval Japan and the Mongol Invasions

Study Map 9-2 on page 267 of the textbook. If the centers of Japanese power were at Kamakura and Kyoto on the island of Honshu during this period, why did the Mongols invade the island of Kyushu? Geographically, why is the city of Kyoto a better strategic location for a center of power than Kamakura?

MAP EXERCISE

Map 9-1: Yamato Japan and Korea (Ca. 500 C.E.)

Identify the following features on Map 9-1 on page 256 of your textbook and place them on the map provided on the next page of this *Study Guide*.

1. Korean Peninsula

2. Kyushu

3. Honshu

4. Shikoku

5. Silla

6. Paekche

7. Koguryo

8. Sea of Japan

9. East China Sea

10. Pacific Ocean

11. Yellow Sea

12. Nara

13. Heian (Kyoto)

Chapter 9

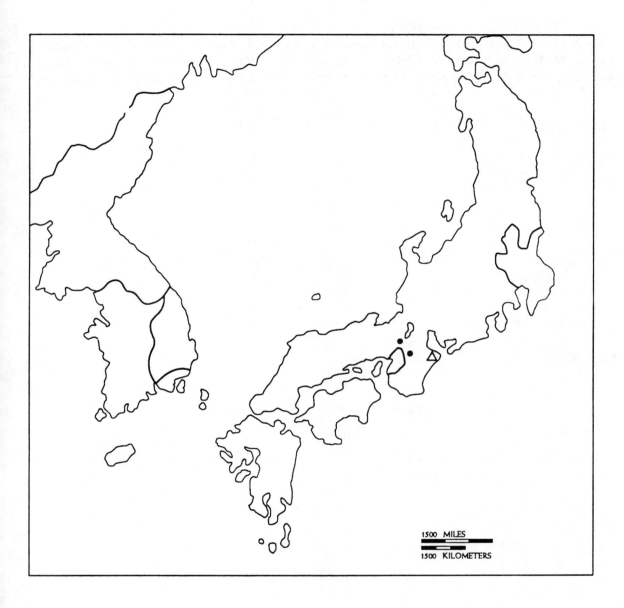

MAP 9-1
Yamato Japan and Korea (ca. 500 C.E.)

Japan: Early History to 1467

127

MULTIPLE CHOICE ANSWER KEY *(with page references)*

1. D (253)	6. D (259)	11. D (265)
2. A (254)	7. A (260)	12. D (266)
3. C (254)	8. B (261)	13. C (269)
4. B (256)	9. A (262)	14. B (270)
5. D (258)	10. B (263)	15. A (274)

10
Iran and India Before Islam

COMMENTARY

This chapter is devoted to an examination of civilization in south and southwest Asia before the penetration of Islam ushered in new eras. In Iran, the Parthian Arsacid rule continued the Iranian imperial tradition begun by the Achaemenids until 223 C.E. Constant warfare against the Romans helped weaken the empire, yet Parthian rule was liberal in granting religious tolerance and laid the groundwork for the nationalistic emphases of the next few centuries.

The Sassanids, who succeeded in 224 C.E., were a Persian dynasty and continued their control over the region until 651. The chapter then details the political rise of Ardashir, the first Sasanid king, and his successors. With the growing shift of the Roman Empire east of Byzantium in the fourth century C.E., the stage of imperial conflict with the Sassanids was set for the next 350 years. The basis of the Sasanid economy was agriculture, but they also taxed the caravan trade. The basic social unit was the extended family and four social classes were recognized: priests, warriors, scribes and peasants. Sasanid aristocratic culture drew on diverse Roman, Hellenistic, Bactrian-Indian, Achaemenid and other native Iranian traditions.

Religion played a significant role in Sasanid life. The government institutionalized Zoroastrian ritual and theology as state orthodoxy. The main opponent to the orthodox faith was Manichaeism. Despite the orthodox victory over Manichaeism, it continued to influence others and contributed to the Mazdakite movement at the end of the fifth century, which demanded a more egalitarian distribution of society's goods. In 528, Mazdak and his most important followers were killed, but the name became symbolic of revolt in later Iranian history.

The chapter then focuses on the Gupta period in India as a "golden age" (320-450). Perhaps the most civilized state in the world at that time, the brilliant leadership of Chandragupta II (375-415) promoted Gupta power to its greatest extent. The empire collapsed in the face of repeated Hun invasions by about 550. The remainder of the empire was shattered by Arab invasions around 1000. The Gupta period and later centuries saw massive literary and artistic productivity in architecture, sculpture and wall painting. Outstanding drama and verse by Kalidash, the "Shakespeare" of Sanskrit letters, flourished at the time of Chandragupta II.

KEY POINTS AND VITAL CONCEPTS

1. <u>Zoroastrianism versus Manichaeism</u>: The Sassanids claimed to be restoring the true faith of Zoroaster after centuries of neglect under Arsacid rule. The greatest figure in this movement was Kirdir in the 3rd century C.E. He made numerous efforts to convert pagans, Christians and Buddhists, but his primary opponents were the Manichaeans. Mani (216-277 C.E.) preached a message similar to, but at crucial points radically divergent from its Zoroastrian, Judaic and Christian forerunners. His preaching was missionary and centered on a dualistic and moralistic view of reality in which he promised the restoration of the original unity of Zoroastrian, Judaic and Buddhist teachings. Kirdir eventually won his struggle against Mani and executed him as a heretic in 227. But Mani's movement spread both east and west, its ideas figuring centuries later in Christian and Buddhist communities.

2. <u>Indian Society</u>: All society was based on a rigid four-class structure and rests on the basic principle that every person is born into a particular station in life and has appropriate duties and responsibilities. The four Aryan classes are priest, noble/warrior, tradesperson and servant. The divisions reflect an attempt to fix the status and power of the upper three groups at the expense of the fourth and "fifth class" of non-Aryan outcasts, who performed the most polluting jobs in society. The three main controls of caste were commensality (take food from or with persons of the same caste or higher), endogamy (marry within one's caste) and trade (practice only the trade of one's group). This caste system has been criticized, but it did give Indian civilization a stability and security for centuries.

3. <u>Hindu and Buddhist Life</u>: The polytheistic Hindu faith stresses the divine presence in multiple forms. In the development of Hindu piety and practice, ardent theism, known as *bhakti* or "loving devotion," is emphasized. Hindu polytheism is not "idolatry" but a vivid affirmation of the infinite forms of transcendence. The major Vedantic thinker was Shankara (d. 820) who stressed a strict "non-duality" of the Ultimate. There were two main developments in Buddhist religious life during the Gupta period: 1) the solidification of the two strands of Buddhism, the Mahayana and the Theravada and 2) the spread of Buddhism from its Indian homeland. The Mahayana goal was to aid all to reach Nirvana through a career of self-sacrifice. The *Theravada*, "the Way of the Elders," focused on the importance of the monastic community; the service and gifts to the monks were a major source of merit for the laity, and merit contributed to a better rebirth. The Mahayana traditions traveled to central Asia and China while the Theravada sect went to Ceylon, Burma and southeast Asia.

4. <u>Iran and India in World Perspective</u>: The common perspective is that these civilizations existed on the periphery of the late Roman and near eastern world of late antiquity. But the focus of political power, cultural creativity and religious vitality throughout most of the early centuries C.E. was based in Byzantine Anatolia, Egypt, North Africa and Syria-Mesopotamia. The western world did not seem to promise much of a future; instead, progress and culture were best embodied in either Sasanid or Gupta culture, or in the far eastern civilizations of China (Han, Sui, and T'ang dynasties) or the Nara and Heian of Japan. A revised perspective would thus see a number of important cultural centers both in the Asian domains and also in Byzantium and in Aksumite Ethiopia.

IDENTIFICATION TERMS

For each of the following, tell who or what it is, about when did it happen, and why it is significant in the history of the period:

Dharma (p. 288):

Mazdakite (p. 285):

Puranas (p. 290):

Kalidasa (p. 286):

Shahanshah (p. 282):

Mahayana Buddhism (p. 291)

Kirdir (p. 284):

Shudra (p. 289):

Bodhisattva (p. 291):

Mani (p. 284):

Jati (p. 289):

Theravada Buddhism (p. 291):

Pahlavi (p. 285):

Bhakti (p. 290):

Chandragupta II (p. 286):

MULTIPLE CHOICE QUESTIONS

1. The last century or so of Parthian rule saw increased emphasis on
   a. foreign traditions in religious and cultural affairs
   b. Iranian traditions in religious and cultural affairs
   c. Roman military techniques
   d. the wealth of Egypt to support its military needs

2. The Sassanids were a
   a. Parthian dynasty   c. Persian dynasty
   b. Aramaic dynasty   d. Gupta dynasty

3. Shapur claimed to be "king of kings" based on his conquest of
   a. Bactria   c. Syria, Armenia, and Anatolia
   b. parts of the Roman empire d. all of the above

4. The greatest Sasanid emperor was
   a. Chosroes Anosharvan   c. Justinian the Wise
   b. Ardashir   d. Kirdir

5. Indian influences on the Sasanid civilization were especially evident in
   a. economic policies   c. medicine and mathematics
   b. historical writing   d. all of the above

6. Sasanid culture was drawn from the
   a. Roman tradition   c. Bactrian-Indian traditions
   b. Hellenistic tradition   d. all of the above

7. Kirdir is important for his
   a. zealotry in support of Zoroastrian theology
   b. conversion to Manichaeism
   c. support of heretical doctrines in defiance of Zoroastrian belief
   d. Buddhist teachings

8. Mani may have been the first person
   a. to edit the Zoroastrian sacred books
   b. consciously to "found" a new religious tradition
   c. to create a "scripture" for his followers
   d. both b and c

9. Manichaeism is significant because
   a. its adherents probably carried the Eastern planetary calendar to the West
   b. it established a new justice system for Islam
   c. its ideas figured in both Christian and Islamic heresies
   d. it refused to challenge Christian and Islamic religious theologies

10. The official Persian dialect of the Sasanid empire was
    a. *Shahanshah*   c. *Kshatriyas*
    b. *Pahlavi*   d. *Jati*

11. The claim of the Gupta era to being India's golden age of culture could be sustained solely on the basis of
    a. its architecture and sculpture   c. its wall paintings
    b. the drama and verse of Kalidasa   d. all of the above

12. In the *Dharmashastra* of Manu, we find
    a. the primary explanation of Hindu theology
    b. the classic statement of the four-class theory of social hierarchy
    c. an engaging work of poetry
    d. a compilation of Gupta dramatic works

13. The caste system
    a. was considered a necessary evil in Gupta society
    b. was only applied to the region of northern India
    c. gave great stability and security to the individual and to society
    d. all of the above

14. Indian reverence for all forms of life is embodied in the principle of
    a. *ahimsa*   c. *bhakti*
    b. *jati*   d. *maya*

15. The two strands of Buddhist religious tradition were the
    a. Mahayana and Theravada   c. *nirvana* and *maya*
    b. *stupas* and *sutras*   d. *bodhisattvas* and *tirthas*

Chapter 10

STUDY QUESTIONS

1. How did the Sasanid empire develop after the fall of the Parthians? What was the role of Zoroastrian orthodoxy? What benefit did the empire receive from the Byzantine state? What were the principal economic bases of the empire?

2. In what ways can the Gupta period (320-450) truly be considered a "Golden Age"? What was the extent of the boundaries during the time? Why did the empire collapse after 550? What was the importance of the movement of culture south to the Tamil?

3. What are the main tenets of the Hindu faith? How did the caste system strengthen the major beliefs of the society and what benefits did it offer? How did Hinduism influence Buddhism during this time period?

4.   What were the main tenets of the Buddhist faith in the Gupta period? Why did the Mahayanan traditions become popular in east Asia and China? What was the importance of merit in the Buddhist faith?

5.   How did the Ghana Empire develop a sound trade relationship in the Sudan? What common traits did all Sudanic kingdoms develop in a political state? What were their major contributions to world history?

6.   How did the rise of the Arab Empire influence Aksumite development? How was Ethiopia able to survive into the twentieth century as an independent kingdom?

DOCUMENT QUESTIONS

1)   A Chinese Traveler's Report on the Gupta Realm (p. 287):

What does the traveler, Fa-Hsien, think about the Gupta realm? What specific things does he admire and what problems does he see? Why are the Chandalas treated so poorly? Fa-Hsien mentions that "Even in cases of repeated rebellion, they only cut off the right hand." What does this tell you about Chinese society in comparison with Gupta values?

2)   A Lyric Poem of Kalidasa (p. 290):

What is the subject of this poem and what message is the author trying to convey to you? Analyze the vocabulary. How are verbs and adjectives used to create interest and drama? How effective is this poetry in creating an impression that the reader will remember?

3) *Devoting Oneself to Krishna (p. 293):*

What is the subject of this excerpt from the *Bhagavad Gita*? How does one attain the highest path to salvation? Why are self-control and knowledge such important components of salvation?

4) *The Buddha Preaching His First Sermon (p. 295):*

Look closely at the picture of the high-relief figure of the Buddha. From the physical appearance of the Buddha alone, what values do you think are important to the Mahayana Buddhist sect? What do the hand gestures symbolize?

MAP ANALYSIS

Map 10-1: International Trade Routes in Gupta and Sasanid Times

Study Map 10-1 on page 288 of your textbook. Note the interconnection between the Sasanid, Gupta, Roman-Byzantine, and Chinese civilizations. Which cities were geographically most important to this international trade? It seems as though the river systems were not utilized in transporting overland goods. Can you offer some explanations for that? What goods and ideas were exchanged along these trade routes?

MULTIPLE CHOICE ANSWER KEY *(with page references)*

1. B (282)	6. D (284)	11. D (286)
2. C (282)	7. A (284)	12. B (288)
3. D (282)	8. D (284)	13. C (289)
4. A (283)	9. C (284)	14. A (290)
5. C (284)	10. B (285)	15. A (291)

11

The Formation of Islamic Civilization (622-945)

COMMENTARY

This chapter discusses the origin and early development of Islamic civilization under the direction of Muhammad. The basic ideals and ideas of the Islamic worldview derived from a single prophetic revelatory event: Muhammad's proclamation of the Qu'ran. The Arab community developed a sense of unity as Muslims, or "submitters" to God. The new civilization was sustained by older diverse cultures that were militarily invaded and yet accepted the new vision of Islamic society.

The origins of Islam centered in the city of Mecca. In this thriving commercial location, center of the busy caravan trade, older tribal values were breaking down. The popular notion that Islam was a "religion of the desert" is largely untrue. The faith centered around its prophet, Muhammad (ca. 570-632). He was raised an orphan and married a wealthy widow. In the midst of a successful business career, he grew increasingly troubled by the idolatry, worldliness and lack of social conscience around him. Muhammad felt himself called by the one true God to "rise and warn" his fellow Arabs about their disregard for morality and worship. Revelation came to him through God's messenger angel Gabriel, and took the form of a recitation (*Qu'ran*) of God's word. The chapter then discusses the Islamic doctrine and the emigration (*Hegira*) of Muhammad in 622 from Mecca to Medina. The basic Muslim vows took shape in Medina: allegiance to the *umma* (Islamic community), honesty in public and personal affairs, modesty in personal affairs, abstinence from alcohol and pork, the five daily rites of worship facing the Kaaba, fasting for one month each year and eventually a pilgrimage to Mecca at least once a lifetime. After Muhammad's death in 632, a political struggle ensued between various factions, since the Prophet never named a successor. Abu Bakr established himself as Caliph (632-634) and held a nominal religious conformity over Arabia. The great strength of the Qu'ranic message was its universalism, and the *umma* or Islamic community grew quickly. There were, however, different interpretations or versions of the *umma*. The most radical idealists were the Kharijites or "Seceders," who believed that Muslim policy must be based on strict Qu'ranic principles and espoused a total egalitarianism; still, they held a rigid moral view and anyone who committed a major sin was no longer a Muslim. A second position was defined largely in leadership terms. Shi'ite Muslims accepted the leadership of Muhammad's son-in-law Ali (which was denied by the Kharijites). They stressed the divinely inspired knowledge of Muhammad and his heirs. As these two contentious groups vied for power, another more moderate group called Sunnis claimed a centrist position and became very influential among pragmatists. They have tended to put communal solidarity above purist adherence to theological positions, and have been inclusive rather than exclusive in their converts and in their maintenance of the faith.

The period from about 700-850 is known as the High Caliphate, a time of political power and cultural vibrancy that saw the legendary rule of Harun al-Rashid (786-809). The vizier was the main advisor to this Abbasid state and mamluk slave troops (mostly from Turkey) formed the core of personal political power. The ideal of full conversion of the Islamic Empire lagged behind the centralization of political power and was never fully realized.

The decline of the empire began in the ninth century with local control being exercised in Spain and parts of North Africa as early as 800. Beginning in 821, Abbasid governors set up independent dynasties in Iran. A Shi'ite family, the Buyids, took over Abbasid rule in 945 and continued as figureheads of Muslim unity until the Mongol invasions of 1258.

The "classical" culture of the Abbasid period was preserved in the tales of *The Thousand and One Nights*. Sophisticated tastes and a thirst for knowledge, any knowledge, were a hallmark of Abbasid rule. Contact with the T'ang empire of China was important in developing the high cultures of the period. Translations of Greek and Sanskrit works were common and familiarized Islamic civilization with the ideas of Galen, Ptolemy, Euclid, Aristotle, Plato and the neo-Platonists. Grammar formed the basis of Muslim learning and Arabic writers specialized in historical and biographical literature. The *hadith*, or reports containing the words or deeds of Muhammad and his companions became the chief source of Muslim legal and religious norms. The avoidance of pictures, icons and overt symbols of public art was an important aspect of the "classical age."

KEY POINTS AND VITAL CONCEPTS

1.   <u>The Message of the Qu'ran</u>: As revealed by God through his Prophet Muhammad, the Qu'ran warns people against idolatrous worship of false gods, immorality and injustice to the weak and less fortunate, the poor, orphans, widows, and women in general. A judgment day at the end of time will see everyone face either punishment in hellfire or external joy in paradise according to how one has lived. The way to paradise is through obedient worship and submission (*Islam*) to God's will thus becoming *Muslim* (submissive). There is but one God (Allah) and Muhammad is his prophet. Yet he was only the last in a long line of prophets chosen to reveal God's message. Others included Noah, Abraham, Moses and Jesus. But Muhammad was chosen to give one final reiteration of God's message.

2.   <u>The Course and Success of Islamic Conquest</u>: In the course of the seventh century, Arab Islamic armies burst out of the peninsula and conquered the Byzantine and Sasanid territories by 640, Egypt by 642 and Iran by 643. Succeeding decades saw conquests of the Berbers, Morocco and much of Spain. Islamic armies were finally checked by the Frank, Charles Martel, at Tours in 732. A combination of factors resulted in this success: 1) Islamic vision of society united Arabs and attracted others as well 2) Religious zeal, especially as time went on, maintained commitment, although too much has been made of Muslim desire for martyrdom in the *jihad* 3) Leadership of the first caliphs and field generals. 4) Liberal ruling policies that were a relief from Byzantine or Persian oppression. These included no military obligations, maintenance of local legal systems, the adjustment of unequal taxation, and relatively little bloodshed or destruction of property.

3.   <u>The New Islamic Order</u>: The Islamic community required a period of political and religious organization after the death of Muhammad. His first successors were chosen on the basis of their superior personal qualities and leadership within their tribes.   Their titles were *caliph* ("successor") or *imam* ("leader") which underscored their political and religious authority. This dual authority was difficult to maintain and the caliphate became a titular office representing political and military unity. Religious leadership devolved upon scholars known as *ulama* ("persons of right knowledge") whose opinions on legal issues and theological doctrine established a general basis of religious order and a workable legal-moral system.

4.   <u>Islamic Civilization in World Perspective</u>: The rise of Islam as a world religious tradition and international civilization is one of the great events of world history. As different as they were, only China compared favorably with or surpassed the Islamic world in terms of political and military power, cultural unity and creativity.   Still, the Islamic empire was culturally heterogeneous and more widely dispersed. The Islamic empire was agrarian-based, but the overall conditions for food production (owing to a general lack of water) were not as favorable as those in China or western Europe. The Islamic achievement was different primarily in that it was consciously an effort to build something new rather than to recapture previous traditions of religion, society or government.

IDENTIFICATION TERMS

For each of the following, tell who or what it is, about when did it happen, and why it is significant in the history of the period:

Muslim (p. 297):

Hajj (p. 302):

mamluks (p. 309):

Ka'ba (p. 298):

umma (p. 300):

ulama (p. 306):

Kharijites (p. 307):

caliph (p. 305):

mahdi (p. 308):

Qur'an (p. 300):

jihad (p. 303):

Sunnis (p. 308):

Harun al-Rashid (p. 309):

imam (p. 305):

Shi'ites (p. 307):

MULTIPLE CHOICE QUESTIONS

1. The basic ideas and ideals of the Islamic worldview derived from a single, prophetic-revelatory event:
    a. the submission of Muslims to the will of *Allah*
    b. Muhammad's proclamation of the Qur'an
    c. the Muslim victory over Charles Martel at the battle of Tours
    d. none of the above

2. The town of Mecca was important because
    a. of its famous sanctuary, the Ka'ba
    b. it was a center of the caravan trade
    c. of its strategic geopolitical location in the center of Arabia
    d. both a and b

3. The notion that Islam was a "religion of the desert"
    a. is largely untrue
    b. enabled it to spread among the desert tribes
    c. allowed it to be carried along the caravan routes
    d. both b and c

4. Muhammad was motivated to establish a new religious tradition because
    a. he was troubled by the idolatry and worldliness of his contemporary society
    b. his poverty was so intense that he had no hope
    c. of the intense political control of the priesthoods by tribal leaders
    d. all of the above

5. The message of the Qur'an was that
    a. the way to paradise lay in proper gratitude to God for forgiveness and guidance
    b. idolatrous worship of false gods would not be tolerated
    c. immorality and injustice to the weak and less fortunate was wrong
    d. all of the above

6. The Hegira refers to
    a. the early Islamic conquest of Egypt
    b. a pilgrimage to Mecca
    c. Muhammad's "emigration" to Medina
    d. the Muslim lunar year

7. Jews, Christians, and other "people of Scripture," who accepted Islamic political authority were
    a. ignored by the Muslim community
    b. tolerated by Islam, but assessed a head tax
    c. excluded from business dealings by Islam, but were not persecuted
    d. considered "unclean" and exiled from Muslim communities

8. Muhammad's successor, Abu Bakr,
    a. lost control of the *Umma* and forced a split between Meccan and Medinan factions
    b. conquered the Byzantine and Sasanid territories of the Fertile Crescent
    c. reestablished nominal religious conformity over the whole of Arabia
    d. both a and b

9. Arab Islamic armies
    a. conquered the lands from Egypt to Iran and united them under one rule
    b. controlled parts of southern France after successfully defeating Charles Martel
    c. never penetrated the Indus region of Sind
    d. both b and c

10. What gave Islamic conquests overall permanence was
    a. the vitality of the new faith
    b. the fact that there was relatively little bloodshed or destruction of property
    c. the appointment of capable governors and astute administrative policies
    d. all of the above

11. The Shi'ites
    a. espoused a total egalitarianism among the faithful
    b. believed that the leadership of the *Umma* belonged to the best Muslim
    c. were called "seceders" who broke away from the leadership of Ali
    d. none of the above

12. The height of caliphal power and splendor came
    a. during the Umayyad rule about 650 C.E.
    b. after the Umayyad decline under the Abbasids about 750 C.E.
    c. under the rule of Ali and the Kharijites about 600 C.E.
    d. under the Seljuk emirs about 1055

13. In the mid-8th century paper manufacture was introduced to the Islamic world from
    a. Europe   c. China
    b. India   d. Egypt

14. Islamic culture took over the tradition of rational inquiry from the Hellenistic world as demonstrated by the
    a. preservation and translation of Greek medical and philosophical works
    b. dominant Greek influence in Islamic architecture
    c. insistence that *imams* learn Greek as a part of their formal schooling
    d. both a and b

15. The *Hadith* was a
    a. significant genre of Arabic writing
    b. compilation of Islamic poetry based on the Arabic ode
    c. collection of reports of the words and deeds ascribed to Muhammad that formed the basic unit of history and biography
    d. book of stories about the pomp and splendor of the Abbasid court

1.	Discuss the importance of Mecca to the development of Arab unity. What role did Medina play? Was Islam a "religion of the desert"?

2.	What were the main reasons for the success of the Arab conquests? What geographic areas were conquered by 732? Why did the older empires fail to stop these invasions?

3.	What are the main concepts of the doctrine of Islam? How is this faith different from Christianity? What is the position of women in the faith? What is the importance of other faiths to this movement?

4.   What was the importance of the *umma* to Muslim society? How were religious minorities and non-Arab converts treated? How did the change of the Islamic capital to Baghdad affect the empire?

5.   What was the impact of the Shi'ite movement on the Islamic faith? Why did it fail to dominate the majority of believers in the faith? What are the main differences between the Shi'ites and the Sunnis?

6.   Describe the main reasons for the decline of the Arab empire. What was the role of the Mamluks in the process of decline? How important was local control to the decline of empire? What were lasting contributions of the Arab empire?

DOCUMENT QUESTIONS

1)   *The Qur'an or "Recitation" of God's Word (p. 301):*

   After reading these excerpts from the Qur'an, what are the powers and characteristics of God? Is Allah loving or wrathful?   How would you compare Him to the Christian God or the Jewish conception of Yahweh? How is Abraham viewed in the Qur'an?

2)   *Traditions from and about the Prophet (p. 313):*

   What religious values and norms are emphasized in these selections? What does the second *hadith* suggest about the Prophet's approach to rights for women? How might traditions such as these serve as moral guidance? What do they suggest about the posthumous role and status of Muhammad in Muslim life?

3) *The Wit and Wisdom of al-Jahiz (p. 312):*

In your opinion, what is the most instructive of al-Jahiz' sayings? *The Book of Proof* is considered a jewel in Arabic literature. Why has it been so revered and what do these bits of wisdom say about the intellectual values of Abbasid society?

4) *The Congregational Mosque (p. 314):*

After studying the photographs of these two mosques, describe the architectural features that are common to both? Compare the Dome of the Rock on page 304. What was the purpose of a mosque and how important is such a building to the practice of Islam?

MAP ANALYSIS

Map 11-1: Muslim Conquests and Domination of the Mediterranean to About 750

Study the map 11-1 on page 303 of your textbook. Note the different stages of conquest and the territory gained in each period. How quickly did the Islamic empire expand when compared to other empires that you have studied such as the Athenian (p. 97), Alexander's (p. 102), the Roman (p. 158), the Han (p. 206), the Mongol (p. 246), and the T'ang (p. 229). Why were the Muslims so successful in their expansion?

MAP EXERCISE

Map 11-1: Muslim Conquests and Domination of the Mediterranean to About 750

By 750, Muslims had come to dominate most areas south and east of the Mediterranean Sea. Identify these locations and place them on the map on the following page of this *Study Guide*:

1.	Persia	7.	Cordoba
2.	Arabia	8.	Mecca
3.	Palestine	9.	Medina
4.	Egypt	10.	Jerusalem
5.	Algeria	11.	Damascus
6.	Spain	12.	Baghdad

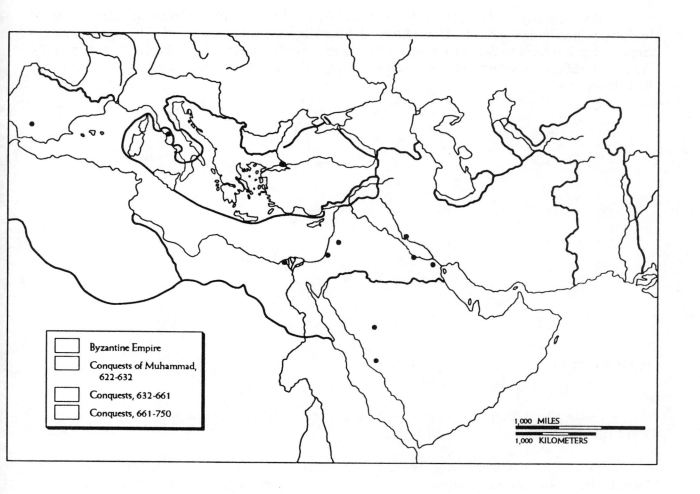

MAP 11-1

Muslim Conquests and the Domination of the Mediterranean to About 750

The Formation of Islamic Civilization ((622-945)   153

MULTIPLE CHOICE ANSWER KEY *(with page references)*

1. B (297)	6. C (300)	11. D (307)
2. D (298)	7. B (300)	12. B (308)
3. A (298)	8. C (302)	13. C (309)
4. A (300)	9. A (302)	14. A (310)
5. D (300)	10. D (303)	15. C (310)

The Early Middle Ages in the West to 1000:
The Birth of Europe

COMMENTARY

This chapter begins the account of the western Middle Ages, the period in which a distinctive European culture began to emerge. It starts with the Germanic and Islamic invasions, contrasts the west with the east (Byzantine civilization), and traces the further development of the church. It then describes the kingdom of the Franks (the Merovingian and Carolingian dynasties), the breakup of the empire built by Charlemagne and finally the development of feudal society.

After the battle of Adrianople in 378, the Roman Empire was unable to resist foreign invasions. Visigoths, Huns and Vandals succeeded in disrupting the empire and upon occasion even invading Rome itself. But the barbarians (who were already Christians) were willing to learn from the people they conquered; the Latin language, Nicene Christianity and Roman law survived.

The eastern empire, also called the Byzantine empire, survived until 1453. It was composed of over 1500 cities, the greatest of which was Constantinople. Imperial policy was always to centralize and conform, although Justinian's revision of Roman law contributed to this process, religious heresy was often a problem. The most important heresy, monophysitism, could not be controlled by persecution or compromise and jeopardized loyalty to the emperor.

In the south, Muhammad (570-632) began the faith of Islam and urged that it be imposed upon fellow Arabs by holy war. Within the next century, the Muslims conquered the southern and eastern coastlines of the Mediterranean and occupied parts of Spain. The Mediterranean was controlled by the Muslims until the eleventh century and east-west trade decreased significantly. But the Muslim advance on the land was stopped in the east by Leo III at Constantinople and in the west by Charles Martel in 732 at Poitiers.

The church survived the invasions as a weakened and compromised institution, but it still had an effective administration and a growing army of monks who proved to be a peculiar strength. The origin and development of monasticism is here related as is the doctrine of "papal primacy" and the religious break between east and west. The break revolved around questions of doctrinal authenticity such as papal primacy, the *filioque* clause of the Nicene Creed and the iconoclastic controversy among other factors.

The chapter continues with the foundation of the Frankish monarchy by Clovis and the ineffective Merovingian rule in Gaul. Effective power was wielded by the "mayor of the palace," a position which was held by such men as Pepin I, Charles Martel and finally Pepin the Short who founded the Carolingian monarchy. In 755 Pepin the Short defeated the Lombards, who had driven the pope from Rome, and he gave the pope the "Papal States" (the land surrounding Rome).

Charlemagne (768-814) continued his father's policies of expansion in the north and protection of the pope in Italy. Charlemagne governed his kingdom through counts who were responsible for maintaining local armies, collecting tribute and administering justice. In order to assure justice and maintain control of his counts, Charlemagne sent out the *missi dominici* who inspected his realm; he himself traveled constantly. A substantial part of the wealth accumulated by conquests was used to attract scholars to Aachen where Alcuin of York was the director of the palace school. The school was intended to upgrade the administrative skills of officials in the royal bureaucracy, but it also led to a modest rebirth of scholarship.

The chapter then chronicles the breakup of Charlemagne's empire after his death. Despite all his efforts, the realm was too fragmented among powerful magnates. After the death of Charlemagne's son, Louis the Pious (814-840), fighting broke out between his sons and the empire was partitioned (Treaties of Verdun, 843 and Mersen, 870) which led to greater fractionalization and weakness.

In the late ninth and tenth centuries, waves of Vikings, Magyars and Saracens attacked Western Europe. Local populations came to be more dependent than ever on local strongmen for security. The Middle Ages were characterized by a chronic absence of effective central government and the constant threat of famine or foreign invasion. "Feudal society" is a term used to describe the adjustments to this breakdown of centralized government. Feudal society is a social order in which a local lord is dominant and the highest virtues are those of trust and fidelity. In the sixth and seventh centuries, individual freemen put themselves under the protection of more powerful freemen. The term "vassalage" means the placement of oneself in the personal service of another who provides protection in return. To support his growing army, a lord would grant land (called a "benefice" or "fief") on which vassals were to dwell and maintain themselves. Vassalage involved fealty to the lord: promising to refrain from any action that might threaten the lord's well-being and to perform personal services for him, of which the chief service was military duty as a mounted knight. As the centuries passed, personal loyalty became secondary to the acquisition of property. Freemen swore allegiance to the highest bidder - a development which signaled the waning of feudal society.

Serfs were farmers who attended the lord's lands; they were subject to dues in kind and their discontent is registered by several recorded escapes. Still the alternative might involve death at the hands of invaders, or the loss of all his possessions and a lifetime of military service to the king. Many preferred to join a monastery or surrender their land to a local lord in exchange for security.

KEY POINTS AND VITAL CONCEPTS

1. Papal Primacy: The bishops of Rome never accepted the institution of "Caesaropapism," the state control of the church which even involved imposing solutions concerning doctrinal quarrels. In the fifth and sixth centuries, they developed the concept of "papal primacy": the Roman pontiff was supreme in the church when it came to defining church doctrine. This idea was radically different from the continuing Caesaropapism of the east. It was destined to cause repeated conflicts between Church and State throughout the Middle Ages. The doctrine of papal primacy was also conceived to combat the competitive claims of the patriarchs of the eastern church. Pointing to Jesus' words to Peter in the Gospel of St. Matthew (16:18), the pope claimed to be in direct succession from Peter as the "rock on which the church was built." This doctrine would cause much controversy and ill-feeling between the western and eastern churches and contributed to the break in 1054.

2. Byzantine Chronology: Byzantine history can be divided up into three distinct periods:
   324-650: From the creation of Constantinople to the rise of Islam.
   650-1070: To the conquest of Asia Minor by the Turks (some would extend this period to 1204 and the fall of Constantinople to the Crusades).
   1070 (1204)-1453: To the destruction of Constantinople by the Turks. In terms of political power and culture, the first period is the greatest.

3. The Franks and the Church: It is significant to note that the Franks were not converted to Christianity until the reign of Clovis (ca. 496). The conversion is controversial but their relationship symbiotic. The Franks as converts to Nicene Christianity (as opposed to Arian) provided protection for the church and in turn received sanction in their victories over other tribes and appropriation of desired territory. By the time of Charlemagne, the church was totally dependent upon the protection of the Franks against the eastern emperor and the Lombards. The coronation of Charlemagne by Pope Leo III in 800 has been viewed as an attempt by the pope to gain stature and assert leverage over the king. It was no victory for the pope, however, as Charlemagne was unrestrained in his Caesaropapism.

4. The Early Middle Ages in World Perspective: Beginning in the fifth century, the barbarian invasions separated Western Europe for centuries culturally from its classical age, a separation unknown in other cultures. Although some important things survived from antiquity in the West (due largely to the Christian church), Western civilization underwent a process of recovering its classical past through a series of "renaissances" that stretched into the sixteenth century. Early medieval China was far more cosmopolitan and politically unified than Western Europe and centuries ahead in technology. In Japan, the Yamato court struggled to unify and control the countryside, as did the Merovingians, and achieved an identity borne of struggle and accommodation. Japan, like Western Europe, remained a fragmented land during this period and there arose too a system of lordship and vassalage based around local mounted warriors called Samurai. Islam's "classical period" of strength and cultural vibrancy overlapped the Carolingian heyday and there were cultural exchanges, as well as conflict between the two societies. Finally, during this period, India was enjoying the high point of its civilization with the Gupta Age (320-1000). The world's great civilizations were reaching a peak during this period with Western Europe lagging behind because of foreign invasions and disruptions that were never experienced in the same magnitude by other world civilizations.

IDENTIFICATION TERMS

For each of the following, tell who or what it is, about when did it happen, and why it is significant in the history of the period:

Alaric (p. 318):

Corpus Juris Civilis (p. 320):

Mayor of the Palace (p. 328):

Attila (p. 318):

Papal Primacy (p. 326):

fief (p. 338):

Justinian (p. 319):

Alcuin of York (p. 333):

Benedict of Nursia (p. 326):

Charles Martel (p. 328):

Donation of Constantine (p. 331):

missi dominici (p. 332):

filioque clause (p. 327):

Clovis (p. 328):

vassal (p. 338):

MULTIPLE CHOICE QUESTIONS

1. Scutage was
   a. a small villa
   b. a monetary payment by a vassal to avoid military service
   c. the obligation of a monk toward the monastic rule
   d. the obligation of the Holy Roman Emperor to protect the papacy

2. During the early Middle Ages, manorialism and feudalism were
   a. destroyed by the barbarian invaders
   b. unsuccessful in ordering society
   c. successful for coping with unprecedented chaos on local levels
   d. successful in establishing trade on a regional level in Europe

3. The German tribes
   a. burst into the Roman Empire all of a sudden, having been pushed themselves by the Huns
   b. were at first a token and benign presence
   c. were often imported by the Romans as soldiers before the Germans became invaders
   d. both b and c

4. As a result of the Germanic invasions of the 4th century, Western Europe
   a. was transformed into a savage land
   b. retained its cultural strength, if not its military control
   c. lost its Roman culture which was replaced by new Germanic institutions
   d. both a and c

5. Arianism had been condemned in 325 at the Council of
   a. Nicea   c. Ferrara-Florence
   b. Chalcedon   d. Constantinople

6. In terms of territory, political power, and culture, which of the following periods in Byzantine history
   was the greatest:
   a. 324-632   c. 632-1071
   b. 1071-1250   d. 1250-1453

7. The imperial goal of the Byzantine emperor in the East was to
   a. centralize government
   b. impose legal and doctrinal conformity
   c. institute a policy reflected in the phrase, "one God, one empire, one religion"
   d. all of the above

8. Islamic invaders differed from Germanic invaders in that Muslims
    a. absorbed and adopted the culture and religion of Rome
    b. were intolerant of Christian and Jewish minorities
    c. ultimately imposed their own culture and religion on the lands they conquered
    d. were not a military match for western armies

9. The Arab invasions and presence in the Mediterranean area during the early Middle Ages
    a. cut off all trade with East Asia
    b. created the essential conditions for the birth of Western Europe as a distinctive cultural entity
    c. contributed to the imposition of eastern trade and cultural influence on the West
    d. provided a protective barrier between Western Europe and hostile Persia

10. One institution remained firmly entrenched within the cities during the Arab invasions:
    a. the *foederati*   c. *Corpus Juris Civilis* of Justinian
    b. the Christian Church   d. Caesaro-papism

11. The doctrine of "papal primacy"
    a. raised the Roman pontiff to an unassailable supremacy within the Church
    b. confirmed the supremacy of bishops within their urban jurisdiction
    c. established papal legitimacy in defining Church doctrine
    d. both a and c

12. The major factor in the religious break between east and west revolved around the
    a. question of doctrinal authority and papal primacy
    b. *filioque* clause of the Nicene-Constantinopolitan Creed
    c. iconoclastic controversy of the early 8th century
    d. all of the above

13. The founder of the first Frankish dynasty was
    a. Charlemagne   c. Clovis
    b. Pepin the Short   d. Charles Martel

14. The head of Charlemagne's palace school was
    a. Einhard   c. Martin of Tours
    b. Alcuin of York   d. Lothar the Wise

15. Under feudalism, the lord's obligations to his vassals included
    a. an obligation to protect the vassal from physical harm
    b. investment of the vassal with a portion of church land
    c. supplying him with his armor and fighting equipment
    d. none of the above

STUDY QUESTIONS

1. Historians have often disagreed as to when the ancient world ended and the Middle Ages began. Do you think the end of the ancient world is characterized by the fall of Rome, or by the triumph of Christianity?

2. Why were the barbarian tribes successful in defeating the Romans militarily? In what ways did the Roman Empire retain its cultural strength? Did the Germanic tribes become more romanized than Rome became germanized?

3. Trace the growth of the Frankish kingdom, including its relations with the church, down to Charlemagne. Then describe Charlemagne, the man and the ruler, and his society. How and why did his empire break up?

4.   Trace the history of Christianity down to the coronation of Charlemagne in 800. What distinctive features characterized the early church? What role did the church play in the world after the fall of the western empire?

5.   How and why was the history of the eastern half of the Roman Empire so different from the western half? What factors contributed to the growth of a distinctive Western European culture?

6.   How and why did feudal society get started? What were the essential ingredients of feudalism and how easily do you think it would be for our modern society to "slip back" into a feudal society?

DOCUMENT QUESTIONS

1)   The Character and "Innovations" of Justinian and Theodora (p. 321):

        In this excerpt from Procopius' *Secret History*, is the author being fair to Justinian and Theodora? Is the *Secret History* a tabloid? How does an historian know when a source is biased and self-serving and when it is telling the truth?

2)   The Great Church of Hagia Sophia (p. 324):

        Study the photographs of this church that was built by the emperor Justinian between 532 and 537. Note that the plain exterior of the church contrasts with the ornate interior. What does this say about the spiritual priorities of the Byzantines? Compare this church with the mosques on pages 296 and 314. What similarities do you find? How do you explain this?

3)   *The False* Donation of Constantine *(p. 329):*

What was the *Donation of Constantine* and why was it so important as a claim to empire? Does the fact that it was fraudulent alter the impact of the document?

4)   *The Carolingian Manor (p. 334):*

What does this accounting say about Carolingian administrative organization? What gave a lord the right to absolutely everything? Was this arrangement a good deal for the stewards and workers of the manor, as well as for the lord?

MAP ANALYSIS

Map 12-1: Barbarian Migrations into the West in the Fourth and Fifth Centuries

Study Map 12-1 on page 319 of your textbook. How many Germanic tribes invaded the Roman Empire? Which tribes penetrated the empire the furthest and had the greatest impact on Roman civilization? Why in particular did the Goths enter the empire? Compare this map with 12-5 on page 337. From what directions was Europe invaded in the 10th and 11th centuries?

MULTIPLE CHOICE ANSWER KEY *(with page references)*

1. B (338)	6. A (319)	11. D (326)
2. C (317)	7. D (320)	12. D (327)
3. D (318)	8. C (322)	13. C (328)
4. B (318)	9. B (325)	14. B (333)
5. A (319)	10. B (325)	15. A (338)

13

The High Middle Ages (1000-1300)

COMMENTARY

This chapter recounts the rise of the German empire, the increasing power of the papacy which led to a crisis between Church and State and their separation, the early crusades, the growth of universities and towns, the society of the High Middle Ages, and political development in England, France, the Holy Roman Empire and medieval Russia.

In 918, Henry I became the first non-Frankish king of Germany. Otto I succeeded in 936, invaded Italy and proclaimed himself king. Otto controlled the church and enlisted it as a part of his rebuilding program, making bishops and giving them land. Otto's successors, however, were so preoccupied with affairs in Italy that their German base began to deteriorate and the church soon became more independent.

A reform movement within the church started at Cluny, a monastery in France. The Cluny reforms were intent on creating a spiritual church and rejected the subservience of the clergy to royal authority. The movement grew to embrace almost fifteen hundred cloisters, and popes devoted to Cluny's reforms came to power during the reign of Henry IV (1056-1106). Pope Gregory VII (1073-1085) prohibited lay investiture of the clergy and ruled that only popes could install bishops. This declaration was a direct threat to Henry's authority over his realm and his protests led to his excommunication by Gregory. After Henry's subservience in the snow at the papal retreat at Canossa in 1077, he regrouped his forces and forced Gregory into exile where he died. The investiture controversy was finally settled in 1122 with the Concordat at Worms, which amounted to a compromise. The real winners in this struggle between Church and State were the local princes.

The early crusades provide an index of popular piety and support for the pope. The First Crusade, proclaimed by Pope Urban II in 1095, captured Jerusalem in 1099 but failed to maintain the territory in the face of rising Arab strength. The Second Crusade also failed to secure the area as did the Third Crusade which saw the divisive effect of the competing monarchs of Europe. Politically and religiously these first crusades were a failure, but they were important in stimulating trade between east and west. The Fourth Crusade, in fact, revealed the interdependence of religion and business.

The western commercial revival resulting from the crusades repopulated old cities and gave birth to new industries. Traders themselves formed a new distinctive social class. They came not from landed nobility, but from poor adventurers. The new rich broke into the aristocracy, and towns became a major force in the breakup of medieval society. Generally, towns and kings allied against the great feudal lords (England was the exception) as kings were able to hire mercenary soldiers, the noble cavalry became militarily obsolete. And as towns and industries attracted serfs from the farms, the nobility gradually lost its once all- powerful economic base.

A renaissance of ancient knowledge in the twelfth century (thanks to Spanish Muslim scholars) contributed to the rise of universities. At first the university was no more than a group of individuals united by common self-interest and for mutual protection. The university was simply a program of study that gave the student license to teach others. The most important universities specialized in particular disciplines such as law or theology and were located at Bologna, Paris, Oxford, Cambridge and Heidelberg.

Four basic social groups were distinguished in the Middle Ages: nobility, clergy, peasantry and townsmen. Noblemen lived off the labor of others; war was their sole occupation and in peacetime they liked hunting and tournaments. Noblemen formed a broad social spectrum, from minor vassals to mighty barons. After the fourteenth century, several factors (population losses, changes in military tactics and the alliance of wealthy towns with the king) forced the landed nobility into a steep economic and political decline.

There were two basic types of clergy: the regular (monks and nuns who lived in cloisters) and the secular (those who worked directly among the laity), who formed a vast hierarchy. Due to the popular reverence for its role as mediator between God and man, the clergy obtained special immunities which townsmen came to resent. After the fifteenth century, governments subjected them to the basic responsibilities of citizenship.

The largest and lowest social group was the agrarian peasantry. There were both servile and free manors. Two basic changes occurred in the evolution of the manor: 1) as the lords parceled out their land to new tenants, manors became hopelessly fragmented and family farms replaced manorial units; 2) the revival of trade and towns made possible the translation of feudal dues into money payments, giving tenants greater freedom. When a declining nobility tried to increase taxes and restrict migration into the city, armed revolts broke out which, although brutally crushed, stand as testimony to the breakup of medieval society.

By modern comparison most medieval towns were but small villages. In the eleventh century the term *bourgeois* first appeared to designate the new merchant groups which formed communities in old Roman towns. These men were suspect within traditional medieval society and advocated a strong central government which would eliminate arbitrary tolls and tariffs that hampered trade. The resulting conflict with the landed nobility led towns to form independent communes and ally with kings.

This chapter also includes a section on medieval women and children. The authors emphasize that the image of women as either subjugated housewives or confined nuns is misleading. Actually, the majority of medieval women were neither. On the one hand, women were dominated by males in almost every aspect of life and were expected to be obedient to husbands whose duty it was to protect and discipline them. On the other hand, women were protected in Germanic law and defended by the church as spiritual equals to males. The vast majority of women were respected and loved by their husbands perhaps because they worked so closely with them in various occupations. Women played a prominent and creative role in workaday medieval society.

The chapter continues with political developments in England emphasizing the invasion by William the Conqueror and his establishment of a strong monarchy. Henry II founded the Plantagenet dynasty and his trials with the clergy and especially Thomas Becket are recounted. Henry's wife, Eleanor of Aquitaine, helped shape court culture and literature in France and England and bore Henry the future kings, Richard the Lion-Hearted and John I. Discontent increased among the English because of high taxation in support of unnecessary foreign crusades by Richard and John. The last straw was the defeat by the French at Bouvines in 1214, which led to a revolt by the English barons and finally the Magna Carta in 1215. This monumental document secured the legitimate powers of the monarchy. The French faced the reverse problem. Feudal princes dominated France from the beginning of the Capetian dynasty (987) until Philip II Augustus (1180-1223). Louis IX (1226-1270) embodied the medieval view of the perfect ruler. His accomplishments in maintaining a unified kingdom, abolishing serfdom, improving the judicial system and establishing a more equitable tax system were widely admired. English expansion stirred France to unity.

Meanwhile the Hohenstaufen dynasty in Germany was unable to establish a stable government. The text details the efforts of Frederick I Barbarossa, Henry VI and Frederick II in their attempts to gain control of Italy and the predictable clash with the papacy which ensued. Frederick II neglected affairs in Germany to such an extent that when he died in 1250, the German monarchy died with him.

Early in the ninth century, Russia was converted to Christianity by Byzantine missionaries. The cultural center of this developing civilization was Kiev which held this position (and defended it against the mongols) until the mid-fourteenth century when Moscow under Ivan I rose as an important power. In 1380, the Mongols were finally defeated in battle and driven out of Russia within the next century.

KEY POINTS AND VITAL CONCEPTS

1. The Investiture Controversy: This controversy involved the selection of bishops and their installation or investiture with the ring and staff which symbolized their office. Traditionally the emperor had done this as a way of assuring the loyalty of his administrators. Pope Gregory VII, inspired by the reforms of Cluny, saw this as an encroachment on papal power. The struggle between Church and State which ensued can also be viewed as stemming from earlier papal assertions of primacy over Caesaropapism. The controversy resulted in a compromise, but in the long run the royal and papal agendas were too competitive for peaceful coexistence. The most bitter clash between Church and State was still to come.

2. The Crusades: The religious and political failure of the Crusades should be stressed with special attention to the Fourth Crusade which saw the sack of Constantinople by the "faithful." In truth, this crusade reveals the interdependence of religion and business; the crusades were important in stimulating new industries, the growth of towns and trade between east and west.

3. Church and State: In this chapter, the clash between Church and State is of central importance in the Plantagenet and Hohenstaufen relations with the papacy. For the most part, the church showed great resiliency in the face of determined opposition from Henry II and Frederick II. Pope Innocent III (1198-1215) made the papacy a great secular power and must stand as one of the most capable leaders of the medieval church. During his reign, the papacy became the efficient ecclesio-commercial complex that was later attacked by reformers. He used the crusade to suppress dissent, especially against the Albigensians. Under Innocent's direction, the Fourth Lateran Council met in 1215 to establish hierarchical church discipline from pope to parish.

4. The Rise of Towns: Feudal society during the High Middle Ages showed signs of collapsing as more serfs left the land for the lure of the city; Louis IX, in fact, abolished serfdom in France. England and France were moving toward centralized monarchies and the transformation from a feudal society to a nation-state more dependent on the wealth and products of its cities had begun. The major exception to this political transformation is Germany which, thanks in large measure to the disastrous reign of Frederick II, remained a bastion of decentralized local rule.

5. The High Middle Ages in World Perspective: During the High Middle Ages, Western Europe concentrated on cultural development and the formation of its political institutions. Everywhere, society successfully organized itself from noble to serf. This was a period of clearer self-definition for the West. Other world civilizations were beginning to depart from their "classical" or "golden" periods. The best lay behind rather than before them. In the late twelfth century, Japan shifted from a civilian to military rule; this marked the beginning of Japan's medieval period. More like Western Europe than China, Japanese women traditionally played a prominent role in royal government and court culture. By the tenth century, Islam had created an international culture and came into greater contact with the West through crusades starting in the late eleventh century. Islam, too, was on the march as it penetrated Turkey, Afghanistan and India, where it encountered a new enemy in Hinduism.

IDENTIFICATION TERMS

For each of the following, tell who or what it is, about when did it happen, and why it is significant in the history of the period:

regular clergy (p. 357):

Domesday Book (p. 364):

Concordat of Worms (p. 347):

secular clergy (p. 357):

Bouvines (p. 364):

Scholasticism (p. 354):

banalities (p. 359):

Magna Carta (p. 350):

Pope Urban II (p. 347):

Cluny (p. 345):

Saladin (p. 348):

lay investiture (p. 345):

simony (p. 345):

"town air brings freedom" (p. 352):

Gregory VII (p. 345):

MULTIPLE CHOICE QUESTIONS

1. The High Middle Ages (1000-1300)
    a. mark a period of intellectual flowering and synthesis
    b. saw the borders of Western Europe largely secured against foreign invaders
    c. saw a revolution in agriculture that increased both food supplies and population
    d. all of the above

2. Otto I won an important victory in 955 at the battle of Lechfeld over the
    a. Bavarians   c. Hungarians
    b. Danes   d. Saracens

3. After 962, the Church
    a. broke away from the control of Otto I
    b. fell under the political control of Otto I
    c. rejected the theory of Caesaro-papism and established an army of its own
    d. both a and c

4. The great Church reform movement of the early 10th century was based at
    a. Otto's court in Swabia   c. Rome
    b. Cluny   d. Chartres

5. Which of the following was a reform instituted by Pope Gregory VII?
    a. the condemnation of abbots who held political office
    b. the prevention of lay investiture of clergy
    c. the rejection of excommunication as a weapon of the Church
    d. both a and b

6. When Henry IV went to Canossa in 1077, he
    a. prostrated himself before the pope and sought absolution
    b. came armed with his barons in order to intimidate the pope
    c. demanded that Gregory relinquish papal control over Saxony
    d. had the German bishops proclaim their independence from Gregory

7. The Concordat of Worms in 1122 required that
    a. the emperor formally renounce his power to invest bishops with the ring and staff of office
    b. the emperor give up the right to nominate or veto a candidate for bishop
    c. the pope invest bishops with fiefs
    d. none of the above

8. The early Crusades were
    a. undertaken for patently mercenary as well as religious motives
    b. successful in controlling the Holy Land politically and militarily
    c. to a very high degree inspired by genuine religious piety
    d. undertaken to destroy the Byzantine power in the region

9. The long-term achievement of the first three Crusades
    a. was to establish a political control over the Holy Land
    b. allowed Christians free and complete access to the Holy Land without hindrance
    c. was that it stimulated western trade with the east
    d. all of the above

10. One of the most important developments in Medieval civilization between 1100 and 1300 was
    a. the victory of the Crusaders over the Infidel
    b. the dominance of vassals over their former lords
    c. the lasting victory of Church over State
    d. revival of trade and growth of towns

11. The University of Bologna was distinguished as the
    a. main training center for government bureaucrats
    b. center for the revival of Roman law
    c. center for church-sanctioned spiritual studies
    d. originator of the college system

12. It was a special mark of the nobility that they
    a. lived on the labor of others
    b. began as great men with large hereditary lands and did not allow others to join their class
    c. resorted to warfare only when they were attacked
    d. rejected the code of chivalry

13. The lord of a manor had the right to subject his tenets to exactions known as
    a. *corvees*   c. *fides*
    b. *banalities*   d. *coloni*

14. Pope Innocent III
    a. made the papacy a great secular power
    b. transformed the papacy into an efficient ecclesio-commercial complex
    c. was a papal monarch in the Gregorian tradition
    d. all of the above

15. In the mid-13th century, Russia fell under the political control of the
    a. Saracens   c. Mongols
    b. Byzantine Greeks   d. Hohenstaufen kings

STUDY QUESTIONS

1.   Discuss the rise of the German empire and the accomplishments of Otto I. Why was he successful? Does he deserve the title, "the Great"?

2.   What were the main reasons behind the Cluny reform movement? What were some of the reforms? How do you account for the success of the movement and what were some of its results?

3.   Discuss the conflict between Gregory VII and Henry IV over the issue of lay investiture, treating in particular the causes of the controversy, the actions of the contending parties and the outcome of the struggle. What was at stake for each of the disputants and what were the ramifications of the struggle?

4. What major development in western and eastern Europe encouraged the emergence of the crusading movement? What were the political, religious and economic results of the crusades? Which do you consider most important and why?

5. What led to the revival of trade and the growth of towns in the twelfth century? What political and social conditions were essential for a revival of trade? How did towns change medieval society?

6. How would you assess the position of women within each of the classes of medieval society? How were their roles and functions different from and similar to those of women in previous ages and those of women in modern times?

DOCUMENT QUESTIONS

1)   *Pope Urban II Preaches the First Crusade (p. 348):*

In this famous speech at the Council of Clermont in 1095, Pope Urban II called for the First Crusade against the Muslim infidel. What are the images he creates of the enemy? How accurate and fair are they? Is propaganda a necessary component of every war?

2)   *The English Nobility Imposes Restraints on King John (p. 365):*

Study these excerpts from Magna Carta. What are some of the basic rights that the nobility demanded from King John? Which of these have become a part of the Bill of Rights for citizens of the United States?

3) *The Investiture Struggle (p. 346):*

Study the 12th century manuscript on page 346 of your text. What is happening? Where do the sympathies of the artist lie? What was the eventual outcome of the investiture controversy?

4) *Gothic Architecture (p. 366):*

Study the picture of the portal of Rheims Cathedral on page 366 of your textbook. What are the main characteristics of "Gothic" architecture? How is this building symbolic of the spiritual strength and social importance of the Church during the High Middle Ages?

MAP ANALYSIS

Map 13-1: The Early Crusades

Study Map 13-1 on page 349 of your textbook. Follow the route of each of the crusades from Europe to the Holy Land. From your analysis, in what ways did the routes differ? Which crusade was the most extensive? Identify in particular the leaders of the Third Crusade? Did it accomplish its goal? Compare the trade routes noted in Map 15-2 on page 423 with the crusade routes on Map 15-1. What conclusions can you draw?

MAP EXERCISE

Map 13-3: Germany and Italy in the Middle Ages

Medieval Germany and Italy were divided lands where disunity and feuding reigned for two centuries. Identify the following locations on Map 13-3 on page 368 of your textbook and place them on the map provided on the next page of this *Study Guide*.

1. Papal States

2. Italy

3. German States

4. France

5. Burgundy

6. Avignon

7. Rome

8. Aachen

9. Augsburg

10. Florence

11. Assisi

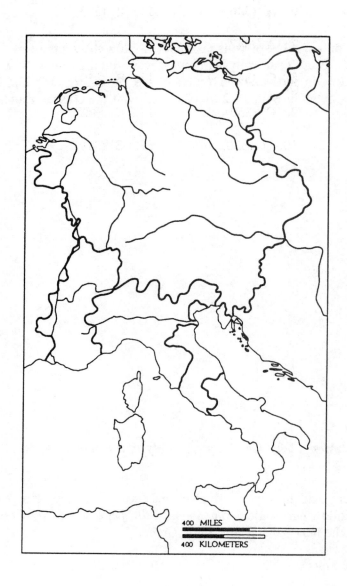

400 MILES

400 KILOMETERS

MAP 13-3
Germany and Italy in the Middle Ages

MULTIPLE CHOICE ANSWER KEY *(with page references)*

1. D (343)	6. A (346)	11. B (353)
2. C (344)	7. A (347)	12. A (355)
3. B (344)	8. C (347)	13. B (359)
4. B (345)	9. C (350)	14. D (367)
5. B (346)	10. D (350)	15. C (370)

The Islamic Heartlands and India (CA. 1000-1500)

COMMENTARY

This chapter surveys the political, social and religious development in the Islamic heartlands of India and Africa over a five hundred year period. Of particular importance is the rise of the New Persian language during the tenth century, which culminated in a rich new Islamic literature, and the political dominance of the Mongols and especially the Turks, who added a substantial linguistic and cultural tinge to the Islamic world.

The chapter then gives a detailed account of religion and society in the Islamic heartlands. Politically, the western half of the Islamic world developed two regional foci: 1) in Spain and North Africa, and 2) in Egypt, Syria, Anatolia and Arabia. The chapter then details western development under the Umayyads (756-1026), the Almoravids and Almohads (1056-1275), and the Fatimids (909-1171) in Egypt. The heirs of the Fatimids and Saladin in the eastern Mediterranean were the redoubtable Mamluk sultans who alone withstood the Mongol invasions from the east. The Saljuqs were the first major Turkish dynasty of Islam. They were based in Iran and extended Islamic control for the first time into central Anatolia in the eleventh century. Culture flourished under Saljuq rule as evidenced by the religious thinkers Muhammad al- Ghazali, and the poet Umar Khayyam.

The building of a vast Mongol empire in the thirteenth century by Genghis Khan and his successors was momentous for the development of Islamic Eurasia. In 1255, Hulagu Khan, a grandson of Genghis, added Turkish troops to his forces and smashed Baghdad's defenses, killing 80,000 people in the process. Hulagu was stopped in 1260 by Berke, a Muslim convert who ruled the Knanate of the "Golden Horde" and allied with the Mamluk sultan. Although the Mongols continued to rule the old Persian empire, the resistance of Berke confirmed the breakup of Mongol unity and of the autonomy of the four Khanates. This situation prepared the way for a Turkish-Mongol conquest from Transoxiania by the Muslim convert, "Timur the Lame" or Tammerlane. Between 1379 and 1405, Tammerlane savagely swept all before him in a frenzy of conquest: Iran, Armenia, the Caucasus, Mesopotamia, Syria, and northern India; his contributions were minimal and his legacy was destruction and political chaos.

Islamic civilization in India was formed by the creative interaction of invading foreigners with indigenous peoples. Wherever Muslim traders went, converts to Islam were attracted by business advantages as well as straightforward ideology and its egalitarian, "classless" ethic. The first Arab conquerors in Sind (711) treated Hindus not as pagans, but as "protected peoples" under Muslim sovereignty. This, of course, did not remove Hindu resistance to Muslim rule. In fact, the chief obstacle to Islamic expansion in India was the military prowess and tradition of a Hindu warrior class (*Rajputs*).

Although the ruling class in India remained a Muslim minority of persianized Turks and Afghans over a Hindu minority, conversion went on at various levels of society. Indian Muslims were always susceptible to Hindu influence in language, marriage customs and caste consciousness; they were never utterly absorbed as earlier invaders had been. Muslims remained a group apart, conscious of their uniqueness in the Hindu world, and proud to be distinct. Southern India contrived to be the center of Hindu cultural, political and religious activity. The kingdom of Vijayanager (1336-1565) was the outstanding example of this identity.

KEY POINTS AND VITAL CONCEPTS

1. The Development of Islamic Religious Sects: The notable developments of this period for the shape of Islamic society were the consolidation and institutionalization of Sufi mystical piety, Sunni legal and religious norms, and Shi'ite sectarianism. Sufi piety stressed simplicity, the ascetic avoidance of temptations, and loving devotion of God. Socially, this piety merged such popular practices as saint veneration, shrine pilgrimage, ecstatic worship and seasonal festivals. Sufi disciples formed brotherhoods, which proved to be the chief instruments for the further spread of the Muslim faith. Shi'ite traditions crystallized between the tenth and twelfth centuries; yet the differences between the diverse Shi'ite groups precluded a unified Shi'ism. Only in Iran, Iraq and the lower Indus did a substantial Shi'ite populace develop. Two Shi'ite groups emerged as the most influential: the "Seveners" or Isma'ilis, who drew on esoteric Gnostic and Neo-Platonic philosophy, and the "Twelvers" who focused on the martyrdom of the twelve *imams* and looked for their intercession on the Day of Judgment. By the eleventh century, most Shi'ites had accepted the latter sect and it has flourished in Iraq, the home of Shi'ite thought. The last major Islamic sect, the Sunnis, melded their traditions by 1000 into a conservative theology reflected by the Hanbalites, who stressed reliance on a literal reading of the Qu'ran and the Hadith.

2. Mongol and Turk Invasions: These invasions in the thirteenth and fourteenth centuries shattered the unity of the Muslim community. The Mongols, however, did not convert Muslim subject populations to their own faith. Instead, their native paganism and Buddhist and Christian followers often yielded to Muslim faith and practice; still, religious tolerance remained the norm under Mongol control. The destructive nature of the conquerors reflected in the sacking of Delhi and Baghdad, required decades of recovery. The lasting legacy of the Mongol invasions was to divide northern India Transoxinia from areas west of Egypt. Muslim culture, however, remained dominant throughout.

3. The Islamic Heartlands and India (1000-1500) in World Perspective: The spread of Islam to India and Africa constitutes only a portion of the history of these particular regions. Yet Islam became truly an international tradition of religious, political, social values and institutions. It did so by being highly adaptable to diverse cultures. Indian traditional culture was not missionary and expansionistic as was that of Islam. Yet Buddhism expanded across much of central and east Asia even while dwindling in its Indian homeland. Christianity, by contrast, was not rapidly expanding, but by 1500 it stood on the brink of internal revolution and international proselytism that began with the voyages of discovery. Most of Africa developed during this period without interference or great influence from abroad. European Christian penetration was just beginning around 1500. In 1000, Europe was almost a backwater of culture and power in comparison with major Islamic and Hindu states, let alone those of China and Japan. At its close, however, European civilization was riding the crest of a cultural renaissance. Over the next five hundred years, western European changes in basic ideas and institutions were much more radical than in other world civilizations.

IDENTIFICATION TERMS

For each of the following, tell who or what it is, about when did it happen, and why it is significant in the history of the period:

Sufism (p. 378):

"Twelvers" (p. 379):

Druze (p. 382):

Madrasa (p. 376):

Rajputs (p. 390):

Tammerlane (p. 386):

Hadith (p. 377):

imam (p. 379):

Ruba'iyat (p. 384):

Hanbalites (p. 377):

Mamluks (p. 382):

ulama (p. 376):

Reconquista (p. 380):

El Cid (p. 380):

Hulagu Khan (p. 385):

MULTIPLE CHOICE QUESTIONS

1. By the mid-10th century in the Islamic world,
   a. centralized caliphal power had broken down
   b. regional Islamic states with distinctive political and cultural configurations now dominated
   c. the stability of the Islamic *ulama* had been maintained
   d. both a and b

2. During the period 1000-1500, what two Asian steppe peoples rose to dominance?
   a. Visigoths and Turks   c. Mongols and Turks
   b. Fatimids and Umayyads   d. Ghaznavids and Saljuqs

3. From the 11th century onward the *ulama's* power and fixity as a class were expressed in the institution of the
   a. *madrasa*   c. *Hadith*
   b. *fiqh*   d. none of the above

4. In the Islamic world, theological positions were most often determined by
   a. sectarian identity   c. orthopraxy (practice)
   b. orthodoxy (belief)   d. both a and b

5. Sufi piety stresses
   a. Islamic law and an observance of Muslim duties
   b. the spiritual and mystical dimensions of Islam
   c. Gnostic and Neo-Platonic philosophy as a foundation of belief
   d. none of the above

6. The two Shi'ite groups that emerged as the most influential were the
   a. *imams* and Batinis   c. Qarmatians and Fatimids
   b. Isma'ilis and Quarmatians   d. Sunnis and Seveners

7. The western half of the Islamic world after the 10th century developed a regional focus in
   a. Spain and Moroccan North Africa
   b. Egypt and Syria
   c. Palestine and Anatolia
   d. all of the above

8. Abd al-Rahman I was important because he
   a. founded the cosmopolitan tradition of Umayyad Spanish culture at Cordoba
   b. upset the stability of Islamic Spain by accentuating the rift between religious factions
   c. closed the mosque-university of Cordoba
   d. both b and c

9. The *Reconquista* or Reconquest refers to the
    a. victory of the Almoravids over the Almohads
    b. victory of Abd al-Rahman I over the Almoravids
    c. victory of Spanish Christian rulers led by El Cid over the Muslims
    d. collapse of Fatimid power throughout the Mediterranean

10. The Almoravids originated as a
    a. religious-warrior brotherhood among Berber nomads
    b. splinter group of the Isma'ili assassins
    c. Sunni religious brotherhood
    d. Sufi religious brotherhood

11. The heirs of the Fatimids and Saladin in the eastern Mediterranean were the
    a. Kipchak Turks   c. Berbers
    b. Mamluks   d. Saljuqs

12. In the mid-13th century, the Mongols were led on the path of conquest in the Islamic world by
    a. Genghis Khan   c. Hulagu Khan
    b. Ghazi warriors   d. Tammerlane

13. Islamic civilization in India was formed by the
    a. Mamluks who invaded Indian lands and imposed Islam on the population
    b. Sufi order which acted as missionaries
    c. creative interaction of invading foreigners with indigenous peoples
    d. both b and c

14. The chief obstacle to Islamic expansion in India was the
    a. military prowess and tradition of a Hindu warrior class
    b. topographical defense afforded by so many rivers and a difficult climate
    c. influence of the great trading city of Kashmir
    d. presence of Mongol armies in the western regions of India

15. Hindu religion and culture
    a. was eliminated in areas of Muslim control
    b. continued to flourish even in areas of Muslim control
    c. broke down with the decline of the *bhakti*
    d. both a and c

STUDY QUESTIONS

1. Describe the political, social and economic conditions in the Islamic heartlands from 945 to 1500. What was the role of the Sunni and Shi'ite sects in this time period? How did the Mongols and the Turks alter the culture in the heartland? Why did Islam survive these outside invasions?

2. Discuss the cultural developments in Spain from 945-1500. Why was Cordoba considered an example of cultural progress? Why were certain Christian and Jewish groups persecuted in this time of great cultural development?

3. What was the impact of Timur the Lame on the Islamic heartland? Why did the Mongols fail to stop this invasion? What motivated the conquests of Timur the Lame?

4.	The period from roughly 1000 to 1500 saw the spread of Islam as a lasting religious, cultural, and political force in world history. Where specifically did Islam spread and how was it introduced to these new regions? Why was it successful?

5.	From the beginning, Muslim leaders faced the problem of ruling an India dominated by an utterly different culture and religion. Discuss the problems of Muslim conquerors. What were their primary obstacles to stable rule and how did they deal with them?

6.	During the Muslim infiltration of India from 1000 to 1500, what happened to the other religious traditions which Islam encountered? Most specifically, address the fate of the Jain tradition, Buddhism and Hinduism.

DOCUMENT QUESTIONS

1)   *Who is the Sufi? (p. 378):*

What qualities or attributes does the Sufi seem to have or seek to develop? According to these selections, what is the Sufi's goal?

2)   *The Alhambra and Islamic Culture (p. 380):*

Study the photograph of the dome in the "Patio of Lions" on page 380 of your textbook. How would you describe the interior architecture and wall decorations? What does this tell you about Islamic culture? What does the fact that the Alhambra was built in Spain indicate about the spread of Islamic civilization?

3)   *The Mongol Catastrophe (p. 386):*

According to the selection from the history of Ibn al-Athir, what was the difference between the Macedonian conquerors led by Alexander the Great and the Mongol invaders? What actions of the Mongols does the author find barbaric? What does he mean by his final sentence?

4)   *How the Hindus Differ from the Muslims (p. 391):*

According to the scholar-scientist, Al-Biruni, what are the three main differences between Muslims and Hindus? Does Al-Biruni think that the differences between the two can be understood and tolerated by the followers of each religion? Does Al-Biruni's last sentence in this selection affect the credibility of his argument?

MAP ANALYSIS

Map 14-1: The Islamic Heartlands (1000-1500)

Study the major ruling dynasties that are noted on Map 14-1 on page 376 of your textbook. It is important to connect the political and cultural activities of these dynasties with their geographical locations. What are "Khanates" and which empire controlled them? How did Ottomans differ from Saljuqs and Mamluks?

MAP EXERCISE

Map 14-2: Islamic Political Sovereignty in 1500

By 1500, Islamic sovereignty had spread widely. Study Map 14-2 on page 388 of your textbook. On the map provided on the next page of this *Study Guide*, shade in the area where there was either Islamic political control or a majority Muslim population.

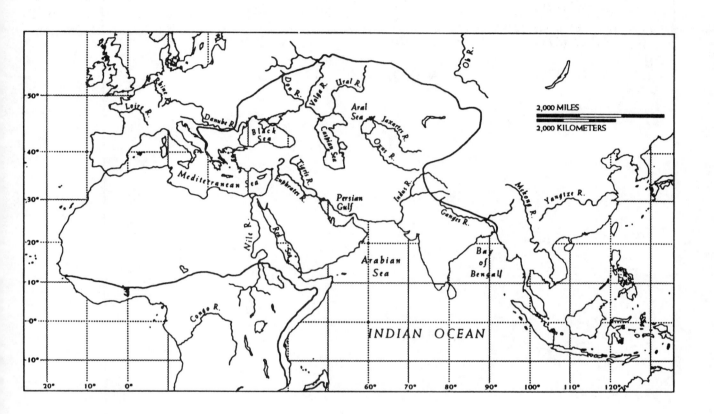

MAP 14-2
Islamic Political Sovereignty in 1500

MULTIPLE CHOICE ANSWER KEY *(with page references)*

1. D (375)	6. B (379)	11. B (382)
2. C (376)	7. D (379)	12. C (385)
3. A (376)	8. A (379)	13. C (388)
4. C (377)	9. C (380)	14. A (390)
5. B (378)	10. A (379)	15. B (392)

15

Ancient Civilizations of the Americas

COMMENTARY

This chapter surveys the development of civilization in the Americas from prehistoric times to the arrival of European explorers in the fifteenth century C.E. The two most prominent centers of civilization in this regions were Mesoamerica, in what is today Mexico and Central America, and the Andean region of South America. At the time of the European conquest of the Americas in the sixteenth century, both regions were dominated by powerful expansionist empires--the Aztecs, or Mexica, in Mesoamerica and the Inca in the Andes. In both regions, Spanish conquerors obliterated the native empires and nearly succeeded in obliterating native culture. But in both, native American traditions have endured, overlaid and combined in complex ways with Hispanic culture.

The chapter then gives a detailed account of the four periods of Mesoamerican history before the Spanish conquest, and initially focuses on the emergence of the Olmec culture that was centered on the lowlands of Mexico's Gulf coast. Most of what is known about the Olmecs comes from the archaeological sites of San Lorenzo and La Venta, flourishing between about 1200 and 400 B.C.E. Probably the best known Olmec works of art are the massive stone heads, some more than twenty tons, that have been found at both San Lorenzo and La Venta. Thought to be portraits of Olmec rulers, these were carved from basalt and transported by raft to the centers. After the Olmec civilization faded after about 400 B.C.E., other regions were rising to prominence. These included the thriving site of Monte Alban that served as the capital of a state that dominated the Oaxaca region.

The Classic Period (150 C.E.- 900 C.E.) was a time of cultural florescence in Mesoamerica. In Central Mexico, it was the rise of Teotihuacan, a great city that rivaled that largest cities of the world at the time. In southern Yucatan, the Maya, developed a sophisticated system of mathematics and Mesoamerica's most advanced hieroglyphic writing. Indeed, Classic Period urban life in Mesoamerica was richer and on a larger scale than in Europe north of the Alps at the same time. The chapter continues with a detailed accounting of each of these important civilizations. Classic Period cities, with their many temples, plazas, and administrative buildings, were religious and administrative centers whose rulers combined secular and religious authority. It was once thought the Classic Period society was composed of peaceful theocracies, without the chronic warfare that characterized Mesoamerica at the time of the Spanish conquest. It is now clear, however, that warfare was common during the Classic Period and that rulers did not hesitate to use force to expand their influence and maintain their authority. The ritual sacrifice of captive enemies was also a feature of Classic Period societies.

Between 800 and 900 C.E., Classic Period civilization collapsed in the southern lowlands. The ruling dynasties came to an end, as did the construction of monumental architecture. By about 900 C.E. a people known as the Toltecs rose to prominence. Their capital, Tula, is located near the northern periphery of Mesoamerica. Aztec mythology glorified the Toltecs, seeing them as the fount of civilization and attributing to them a vast and powerful empire to which the Aztecs were the legitimate heirs. Toltec iconography, which stresses human sacrifice, death, blood, and military symbolism, supports their warlike reputation. This civilization was short-lived. By about 1100, Tula was in decline and its influence gone.

The people commonly known as the Aztecs referred to themselves as the Mexica, a name that lives on as Mexico. Because of the dramatic clash with Spanish adventurers that brought their empire to an end, we have more direct information about the Aztecs than any other pre-conquest Mesoamerican people. Aztec conquests ultimately included almost all of central Mexico. After a conquest, the Aztecs usually left the local elite intact and in power, imposing their rule indirectly. But they demanded heavy tribute in goods and labor. Tribute imposed on defeated tribes undermined the stability of the Aztec empire by creating hatred and dissent. The Aztec capital, Tenochtitlan, was wealthy, but ultimately at risk, since it was "a beautiful parasite, feeding on the lives and labor of other peoples and casting its shadow over all their arrangements." The chapter continues to discuss Aztec society in some detail.

The Andean region of South America--primarily modern Peru and Bolivia--had, like Mesoamerica, a long history of indigenous civilization when Spanish Conquerors arrived in the sixteenth century. The chapter then details the seven periods of Andean civilization from 3000 B.C.E.E to the destruction of the Inca Empire in 1532. Of particular interest are the coastal cultures at Chavin de Huantar about 800 B.C.E., the Nazca culture, which flourished from about 100 B.C.E. to about 700 C.E., and the Moche, which flourished from about 200 to 700 C.E. on the north coast of Peru. The Moche were the most sophisticated smiths in the Andes. They developed innovative alloys, cast weapons and agricultural tools, and used the lost-wax process to create small, intricate works.

By the early sixteenth century, the Incas, expanding from their highland center in Cuzco, had established the most extensive native empire the continent ever saw and ruled several million native Americans over territory that now includes portions of Ecuador, Peru, Bolivia, and Chile. The Incas were not so numerous a people as the Aztecs, nor did they possess so large a military. Instead, the Incas were masters of organization. They compelled conquered tribes to fight for them by richly rewarding successful warrior and by treating well the conquered tribes who aided them. In this regard the Incas frequently ruled indirectly by coopting local rulers into their service. The Incas sent colonists of their own into conquered regions and undertook resettling some conquered peoples. They required resettled peoples and the elites of conquered peoples to speak Quechua, their own unwritten language, with the result that it remains spoken extensively event today among Indians of the Andean region. A relatively large bureaucracy helped the Incas to institute these policies effectively. By the time the Spanish arrived, the Incas were engaged in a civil war between rival claimants to the throne. The chapter goes on to discuss the agricultural and engineering achievements of the Incas, as well as the Incan economy, society, and political administration, all supported by an extensive network of roads.

KEY POINTS AND VITAL CONCEPTS

1. Problems in Reconstructing the History of Native American Civilization: Several difficulties confront scholars trying to understand these ancient civilizations. One is simply the nature of the evidence. Andean civilizations never developed writing, and in Mesoamerica much of the written record was destroyed by time and conquest, and what remained was until recently undeciphered. Archaeology has been successful at teasing out many details of the American past, but we fortunately have narrative accounts of the history and culture of the Aztecs and Inca from Spanish missionaries and officials in the wake of the conquest. But it is almost impossible to know how much they are colored by the conquest and the expectations of the conquerors. Indeed, scholars seeking to understand preconquest Native American civilization and reconstruct its history have had to rely on the language and categories of European thought to describe and analyze peoples and cultural experiences that had nothing to do with Europe.

2. The Mesoamerican Calendar: The Mesoamerican calendar and the earliest evidence of writing has been found in the Valley of Oaxaca at Monte Alban. The calendar is based on two interlocking cycles, each with its own day and month names. One cycle of 365 days was tied to the solar year and the other of 260 days when combined produced a "century" of fifty-two years. At the time of the Spanish conquest, all the peoples of Mesoamerica used this fifty-two year calendrical system. Only the Maya developed a calendar based on a longer time period, anchored--like the Jewish, Christian, or Muslim calendars--to a fixed starting point in the past.

3. The Collapse of Mayan Civilization: The cause of the collapse of Classic Period Mayan civilization about 800 C.E. has long been a subject of intense speculation, but the factors that may have contributed to it are becoming clearer. Among them are intensifying warfare, population growth, increased population concentration, and attempts to increase agricultural production that ultimately backfired. Since ambitious building projects continued right up to the collapse, some scholars believe that as a growing proportion of the population was employed in these projects, fewer were left to produce food. Over-farming may then have led to soil exhaustion. Clearly the Maya exceeded the capacities of their resources, but exactly why and how remain unknown.

4. Aztec Religion and Human Sacrifice: Human sacrifice on a prodigious scale was central to Aztec ideology, since Huitzilopochtli, the sun god, required the sustenance of human blood to sustain him as he battled the moon and stars each night to rise again each day. On major festivals, thousands of victims might perish. Small children were sacrificed to the rain god Tlaloc, who, it was believed, was pleased by their tears. Although human sacrifice had long been characteristic of Mesoamerican societies, no other Mesoamerican people practiced it on the scale of the Aztecs. Human sacrifice certainly must have intimidated subject peoples and may also have had the effect of reducing the population of fighting age men from conquered provinces, and with it the possibility of rebellion. Together with the heavy burden of tribute, human sacrifice may also have fed resentment and fear, explaining why so many subject people were willing to throw in their lot with Cortes when he challenged the Aztecs.

5. <u>Ancient Civilizations of the Americas in World Perspective</u>: Civilization in the Americas before 1492 developed independently of civilization in the Old World. While King Solomon ruled in Jerusalem, the Olmec were creating their monumental stone heads. As Rome reached it apogee and then declined, so did the great city of Teotihuacan in the Valley of Mexico. As Islam spread from its heartland, the rulers of Tikal brought their city to its greatest splendor before its abrupt collapse. Mayan mathematics and astronomy rivaled that of an other peoples of the ancient world. The encounter between Old World and New, however, would prove devastating for American civilization. The technology that allowed Europeans to embark on the voyages of discovery and fight destructive wars among themselves caught the great native empires unprepared. Uncertain how to respond to these aggressive foreigners, they succumbed.

IDENTIFICATION TERMS

For each of the following, tell who or what it is, about when did it happen, and why it is significant in the history of the period:

Olmec Heads (p. 399):

Teotihuacan (p. 401):

Tikal (p. 403):

Long Count (p. 404):

Chichen Itza (p. 400):

Tenochtitlan (p. 407):

Huitzilopochtli (p. 411):

Calpulli (p. 411):

Pochteca (p. 411):

Chinampas (p. 411):

Chavin de Huantar (p. 413):

Nazca culture (p. 414):

Moche culture (p. 415):

Chimu Empire (p. 416):

MIta (p. 418):

MULTIPLE CHOICE QUESTIONS

1. Difficulties confront scholars trying to understand the ancient civilizations of the Americas because
   - a. Andean civilizations never developed writing
   - b. Mesoamerican civilizations never developed writing
   - c. Andean writing displays a pro-Spanish bias
   - d. most of the evidence is from an oral tradition

2. Mesoamerica extends from
   - a. central Mexico into Central America
   - b. Central America to Brazil
   - c. North America to Mexico
   - d. Chile north to Panama

3. The "classic" or high point of Mesoamerican civilization occurred during which period?
   - a. 2000 B.C.E. - 150 C.E.
   - c. 150 - 900 C.E.
   - b. 900 - 1521 C.E.
   - d. 800 - 2000 B.C.E.

4. The people of the Americas never developed the wheel because they
   - a. were inferior engineers
   - c. had no ready access to wood and iron
   - b. had no large draft animals
   - d. were nomadic hunter-gatherers

5. The best known Olmec works of art are
   - a. pyramids
   - c. massive stone heads
   - b. clay pottery
   - d. obsidian statues

6. The monumental architecture at San Lorenzo suggests that Olmec society
   - a. was dominated by an elite class of ruler-priests
   - b. maintained social equality between the sexes
   - c. was monotheistic
   - d. both a and c

7. The Mesoamerican Calendar is based on
   - a. a lunar year of 260 days
   - b. two interlocking solar cycles
   - c. a century of 35 years
   - d. both b and c

8. The Pyramid of the Sun is closely associated with which civilization?
   - a. Teotihuacan
   - c. Guatemala
   - b. Inca
   - d. Maya

9. Historians know more about the Maya civilization because of
   - a. Aztec records
   - b. rapid advances in the decipherment of Maya writing
   - c. Inca trade records
   - d. both a and b

10. The Toltec civilization
    a. lasted for over a thousand years
    b. influenced the Aztecs in terms of religion and mythology
    c. held a powerful empire that included the Maya centers
    d. all of the above

11. After a conquest, the Aztecs
    a. destroyed their enemy's cities
    b. did not demand tribute in goods or labor
    c. left the local elite in power and ruled indirectly
    d. both b and c

12. Central to Aztec ideology was
    a. the death of the river god
    b. the ressurection of four sun goddesses
    c. human sacrifice
    d. flowers that signified the birth of civilization

13. Which of the following is the correct chronological order for Andean civilizations?
    a. Chavin de Huantar, Moche, Chimu, Inca
    b. Moche, Chimu, Inca, Chavin de Huantar
    c. Chimu, Moche, Chavin de Huantar, Inca
    d. Chavin de Huantar, Chimu, Moche, Inca

14. When Francisco Pizarro arrived in 1532, the Incan Empire was
    a. in decline
    b. one of the largest states in the world
    c. confined to the center of Machu Picchu
    d. not yet free from the control of the Chanca people

15. The Incas ruled their empire by
    a. extracting tribute from their subject peoples
    b. relying on various forms of labor taxation
    c. employing people in full-time state service
    d. both b and c

STUDY QUESTIONS

1. What are some of the difficulties that have confronted scholars trying to understand the ancient civilizations of the Americas? What is the nature of the evidence? What role have European words and rivalries played in the interpretation of American civilizations?

2. Discuss the Olmec centers of San Lorenzo and La Venta. What have archaeologists found there that tell us about the Olmec civilization? Refer specifically to the art, architecture and public services.

3. Discuss the importance of the Maya culture and its influence in southern Mesoamerica. What was life like in such Maya centers as Tikal and Chichen Itza? What were the greatest contributions of the Maya?

4.   The text notes that the Aztecs had an "extractive empire." What does this mean? How did the organization of the Aztec empire and the treatment of subject peoples differ from that of the Incas?

5.   The practice of human sacrifice is of particular importance in Mesoamerican civilizations. What was the religious significance behind it and how was it practiced particularly by the Aztecs? Was human sacrifice a moral evil? What did the Sapnish think? Could the Spanish justify their obliteration of the Aztec civilization in an ethical sense?

6.   Both the Aztec and Inca empires fell in the early sixteenth century when confronted with Spanish forces of a few hundred men. Why were the American empires defeated?

DOCUMENT QUESTIONS

### 1)	A Maya Myth of Creation (p. 405):

This segment of the creation myth is from the *Popol Vuh*, a compendium of Maya mythology and history. How does this myth describe the world before creation? Who existed before creation and what did they do to create the earth? Is this a sophisticated myth?

### 2)	A Spaniard Describes the Glory of the Aztec Capital (p. 408):

This famous description of Tenochtitlan by Bernal Diaz demonstrates the glory of the Aztec capital. What achievements of the Aztecs especially astonished Diaz? How was the king, Monteczuma, attended and what does this say about the social structure of the Aztecs? How does this account help explain the Spanish conquest?

3) *Nezahualcoyotl of Texcoco Sings of the Giver of Life (p. 410):*

Nezahualcoyotl was ruler of Texcoco from 1402-1472 and was admired as a philosopher-king. In this song, what does he mean by He Who invents Himself? What kind of relationship can humans achieve with this being? Why does the singer compare seeking the Giver of Life with seeking someone among flowers? How does this song remind you of the thought and religious traditions of China, India, Egypt and Greece?

4) *The Inca City of Machu Picchu (p. 417):*

After studying this photograph of the Incan capital, what can you say about the sophistication of the Incan civilization? How difficult would it be to rule an empire from a location high in the Andes? How difficult was it for the Spaniards to conquer the Incas?

MAP ANALYSIS

Map 15-2: The Aztec and Inca Empires

Study Map 15-2 on page 409 of your textbook. How did the Aztecs and Incas differ in administering their empires and what did it take to consolidate them? Why did they fall so easily to the Spanish conquerors in the 16th century? How did geographical considerations impact the Spanish conquest and maintenance of the former Aztec and Inca empires?

MULTIPLE CHOICE ANSWER KEY *(with page references)*

1. A (398)	6. A (399)	11. C (407)
2. A (398)	7. B (400)	12. C (410)
3. C (398)	8. A (402)	13. A (416)
4. B (399)	9. B (402)	14. B (417)
5. C (399)	10. B (407)	15. D (418)

16

The Late Middle Ages and the Renaissance in the West (1300-1527)

COMMENTARY

This chapter discusses the political, social and economic decline of the fourteenth century and renewal in the fifteenth century. Topics include the Hundred Years' War, the Black Death, relations between Church and State, development of England, Spain and France into centralized nation-states, as well as the history of Germany and Italy. The treatment of Italy includes the renaissance of classical learning and the growth of Humanism.

The underlying causes of the Hundred Years' War included English possession of French lands along the coast: French support of the Bruces of Scotland (who were fighting to end English overlordship of Scotland), a quarrel over Flanders and the strong hereditary claim of King Edward III of England to the French throne. The war lasted from 1337-1453, with 68 years of at least nominal peace and 44 of active fighting. France had a much larger population and was wealthier than England, but received poor leadership from their kings and, unlike England, the country was internally divided. After early English victories, French national sentiment was spurred to unprecedented heights by Joan of Arc, and a unified France progressively forced the English back. By 1453, the English held only their coastal enclave in Calais.

The bubonic plague known as the "Black Death" hit a Europe in 1347 which had been weakened by decades of overpopulation, economic depression, famine and bad health. Raging from 1347-1350, it killed as much as 2/5 of the population of western Europe. As a result of the plague, agricultural prices fell while the cost of manufactured goods rose. Noble landowners suffered as per capita income in the cities increased. Trade guilds became powerful and monarchs were able to continue the process of governmental centralization.

In the thirteenth century, the church was being undermined by internal religious disunity and by the denial of imperial power, for the papacy was now on the defensive against its old anti-imperial allies. Pope Boniface VIII (1294-1303) tried to maintain the papal monarchy of the early thirteenth century, but a French army sent by King Philip IV surprised the pope; Boniface was beaten up and almost killed. There was no lasting papal retaliation. Pope Clement V (1305-1314) moved his permanent residence to Avignon (called the "Babylonian Captivity") and the papacy remained subservient to the French king from 1309 to 1377. From 1378 to 1417, there occurred the Great Schism in the church which saw rival popes and division of support among secular leaders. With the papacy in such chaos, there followed an attempt at conciliar government for the church. The chapter then details this movement and focuses in particular on the Councils of Constance (1414-1417) and Basil (1431-1449). By mid-century, the papacy had recovered adequately to assume a controlling role in church councils.

Renaissance society took distinctive shape within the cities of Italy. There were five major states: Milan, Florence, Venice, the Papal States and the Kingdom of Naples. These states had various types of government, but most evolved into despotisms after near-anarchic social conflict. All of them possessed great wealth, the main requirement for patronage of the arts and letters.

Humanism was the scholarly study of the Greek and Latin classics and the ancient Church Fathers, both for their own sake and in hope of a rebirth of ancient values. Humanists believed that much of traditional education was useless: education should promote individual virtue and public service. The chapter then details intellectual development such as the neo-Platonism of Ficino and the famous oration of Pico Della Mirandola. The art of the period is also discussed with special emphasis on the realism of Leonardo da Vinci, Raphael, Michelangelo and Giotto.

The internal cooperation of Italy's city-states, which had been maintained during the fifteenth century, broke down in 1490. Threatened by attack from Naples, Florence and the Papal States, the Milanese despot Ludovico asked for French help. A series of three French invasions ensued which resulted in Spanish intervention as well. Italy was left a shambles. Machiavelli became convinced that Italian political unity and independence were ends worth any means. He wrote *The Prince* in 1513 to encourage the emergence of a strong ruler from the Medici family. Italy, however, remained divided.

Because of the Hundred Years' War and the Schism in the church, the nobility and the clergy were in a decline in the Late Middle Ages. The bonds of feudal society were finally broken and sovereign states arose. Monarchies began to create bureaucracies which administered the realm and collected taxes which were increased to support the new standing armies. The chapter then details the rise of France under Louis XI, the unification of Spain under Ferdinand and Isabella, the conflict in England with the "War of the Roses," and the establishment of the Tudor monarchy in 1485 under Henry VII. In Germany, an agreement known as the Golden Bull established a seven-member electoral college in 1356 which also functioned as a transregional administrative body. But Germany remained the most disunited of late medieval countries.

KEY POINTS AND VITAL CONCEPTS

1.   The Black Death: One of the great determinants of change in history is disease. The social and economic results of the plague were wide-ranging and included fluctuation of agricultural prices and city income, as well as a decline in trade and the quality of goods produced. Politically, it is important to note that the powers of the two great containers of monarchy in the Middle Ages, the church and the nobility, suffered greatly in numbers and prestige from the effects of the plague. Monarchs were able to progress toward the centralization of their governments and economies.

2.   Relations Between Church and State: The late 13th and 14th centuries were a period of chaos for the church. The victim of attacks by local political factions, the papacy lost respect because of its transfer to Avignon, the Schism which followed, the impact of the Conciliar Movement, the corruption of Alexander VI and others, and the French involvement in Italy. In the long run, the sword of the secular arm proved more than a match for the medieval church.

3.   The Renaissance: Renaissance is a French term meaning "rebirth" which describes the dawning of a new era which took its inspiration from classical antiquity. The revival of learning and emphasis upon man and his unique abilities and beauty contrasts with the medieval emphasis upon the glory of God and the sinfulness of man. The "rebirth" of Western Civilization implies that the Middle Ages were years of decline and sterility. Although true in some ways, medieval civilization can certainly be viewed as progressive and even exceptional in the establishment of trade routes, commerce and technology. The Late Middle Ages was a period of "creative breakup".

4.   Renaissance Slavery: Although the Renaissance is often viewed as a progressive era, slavery flourished as extravagantly as art and culture. As a result of the ravages of the Black Death (1348-1350) on the free labor pool, the demand for slaves soared and they were imported from Africa, the Balkans, Crete, and the lands surrounding the Black Sea. Slavery was multicultural and represented whites and Asians as well as Russians, Greeks and Africans. In addition to widespread domestic slavery, collective plantation slavery also developed in the west in the savannas of Sudan and on the Venetian estates in the eastern Mediterranean. Although owners had complete dominion over their property, domestic slaves at least were generally well treated and integrated into households.

IDENTIFICATION TERMS

For each of the following, tell who or what it is, about when did it happen, and why it is significant in the history of the period:

Edward III (p. 426):

Avignon (p. 433):

Lorenzo de Medici (p. 435):

Joan of Arc (p. 428):

Petrarch (p. 437):

Humanism (p. 436):

Jacquerie (p. 428):

Lorenzo Valla (p. 438):

The Prince (p. 443):

Philip IV (p. 432):

Great Schism (p. 433):

Leonardo da Vinci (p. 441):

Unam Sanctam (p. 432):

Alexander VI (p. 443):

Council of Constance (p. 433):

MULTIPLE CHOICE QUESTIONS

1. The Late Middle Ages has been described as a period of
   a. both waning and harvest
   b. creative breaking up
   c. constriction and expansion
   d. all of the above

2. The underlying cause for the Hundred Years' War between France and England was the
   a. fact that the English king was a vassal of the French king
   b. French support of the Bruces of Scotland
   c. decades of prejudice and animosity between the French and English people
   d. all of the above

3. At the outset of the Hundred Years' War,
   a. England was wealthier
   b. France had military superiority
   c. France had a greater population base
   d. both a and b

4. The Treaty of Troyes in 1420
   a. provided for the death of Joan of Arc
   b. proclaimed Henry V the successor to the French throne
   c. disinherited Henry V from all lands in France
   d. both a and b

5. Joan of Arc gave the French people and armies
   a. an alliance with Flanders
   b. the support of the Church and papal financial contributions
   c. a legitimate heir to the throne of France
   d. a unique inspiration and mystical confidence in the concept of France as a nation

6. Although the Hundred Years' War devastated France, it
   a. resulted in the transfer of English culture throughout France
   b. hastened the transition in France to a feudal monarchy
   c. awakened the giant of French nationalism
   d. resulted in lasting trade contacts with England

7. The Black Death
   a. was preceded by years of famine which weakened the populace
   b. followed the trade routes into Europe from England
   c. devastated primarily the rural population of Europe
   d. was preceded by a gradual decline in population

8. Among the social and economic consequences of the plague were a
    a. shrunken labor supply
    b. rise in agricultural prices
    c. decline in the price of luxury and manufactured goods
    d. all of the above

9. The papal bull, *Unam Sanctam*, declared that
    a. the Holy Roman Emperor could establish national churches in his realm
    b. a new Crusade was necessary in order to unify Europe spiritually
    c. temporal authority was "subject" to the spiritual power of the Church
    d. none of the above

10. After the humiliation of Pope Boniface VIII at the hands of agents of Philip IV
    a. the Holy Roman Empire was dissolved
    b. the popes retreated to Avignon for sanctuary
    c. vassals of the English king invaded France in support of the pope
    d. never again did popes so seriously threaten kings and emperors

11. Which of the following is in the correct chronological order?
    a. Babylonian Captivity, Conciliar Movement, Great Schism
    b. Babylonian Captivity, Great Schism, Conciliar Movement
    c. Great Schism, Babylonian Captivity, Conciliar Movement
    d. Conciliar Movement, Great Schism, Babylonian Captivity

12. Who of the following was the creator of the famous painting, *The School of Athens*?
    a. Giotto   c. Leonardo
    b. Raphael   d. Michelangelo

13. In Renaissance Florence, the *popolo grasso* referred to the
    a. nobles and merchants who traditionally ruled the city
    b. poor masses who lived from hand to mouth
    c. emergent new-rich merchant class
    d. none of the above

14. Humanists were
    a. advocates of a liberal arts program of study
    b. rich merchants who either wrote poetry or painted
    c. supporters of the Church
    d. scholars who looked to the present rather than the past for inspiration

15. Pope Julius II
    a. was known as the "warrior pope"
    b. invaded France in order to control portions of Switzerland
    c. was also a writer of satires
    d. all of the above

STUDY QUESTIONS

1. Consider the Black Death. What were its causes and why did it spread so quickly throughout western Europe? Where was it most virulent? What were the results of the Black Death and how important do you think disease is in changing the course of history?

2. What was the "Babylonian Captivity" and why did it take place? Discuss its importance with regard to the state of the papacy and the resulting Great Schism. How did the church become divided and how was it reunited? Why was the Conciliar Movement a set-back for the papacy?

3. Can you infer from the actions of the great medieval popes what Europe would have looked like religiously and politically had they been able to carry out their reform programs? What institutions, traditions, etc., stood in the way of a king determined to increase his power? Which is the stronger and more lasting force -- the Church or the State?

4.	"The church as an institution was threatened from both those who believed too much and those who believed too little." Comment on this statement.

5.	How would you define "Renaissance Humanism"? In what ways was the Renaissance a break with the Middle Ages and in what ways did it owe its existence to medieval civilization?

6.	Who were some of the famous figures of the Italian Renaissance and what did these individuals have in common which might be described as "the spirit of the Renaissance"?

DOCUMENT QUESTIONS

1)   Joan of Arc Refuses to Recant Her Beliefs (p. 429):

According to this trial record, what was Joan of Arc's argument in defense of her actions? Do you find it compelling? Why was Joan executed and what were her contributions to the history of France? Was Joan of Arc more powerful dead than alive?

2)   Petrarch's Letter to Posterity (p. 437):

What do you learn about Petrarch from this excerpt of his famous letter? What did he value in life? Are these values particular to his age or more universal in application?

3)   *Christine de Pisan Instructs Women (p. 439):*

According to Christine de Pisan, what are a woman's responsibilities in running a household? How should she support her husband? Would the church have approved of her advice?

4)   *Why the Princes of Italy Lose their Power (p. 445):*

According to Machiavelli, why do rulers fail? To what extent are human affairs governed by Fortune and to what extent are human beings responsible for their own actions?

MAP ANALYSIS

Map 16-2: Spread of the Black Death

After studying Map 16-2 on page 431 of your textbook, determine the origin of the Black Death and its introduction to Europe. How fast did the disease travel? Where was it most virulent? In particular, compare the spread of the plague on this map with Map 13-2 on page 351 of your textbook. What similarities can you see, especially in Spain and France? What does this tell you about how the disease spread?

MAP EXERCISE

Map 16-3: Renaissance Italy

Renaissance Italy was divided into several self-contained city-states ruled by despots and co-existing under treaties. Identify the following locations on Map 16-3 on page 436 of your textbook and place them on the map provided on the next page of this *Study Guide*.

1) Kingdom of Naples

2) Duchy of Milan

3) Papal States

4) Republic of Genoa

5) Republic of Florence

6) Republic of Venice

7) Adriatic Sea

8) Tyrrhenian Sea

MAP 16-3
Renaissance Italy

MULTIPLE CHOICE ANSWER KEY *(with page references)*

1. D (425)	6. C (429)	11. B (433)
2. D (426)	7. A (430)	12. B (441)
3. C (426)	8. A (430)	13. C (435)
4. B (428)	9. C (432)	14. A (436)
5. D (428)	10. D (433)	15. A (443)

Chapter 16

17

The Age of Reformation and Religious Wars

COMMENTARY

This chapter discusses the political, social and particularly religious developments of the fifteenth and sixteenth centuries. The chapter focuses particularly on the northern Renaissance and the independent lay and clerical efforts to reform religious practice. It also delves into the various ideas of Martin Luther, Ulrich Zwingli, John Calvin, Henry VIII and other religious and political reformers. It then assesses the effect of the Reformation on society, religion and education.

In the fifteenth century, commercial supremacy was transferred from the Mediterranean and the Baltic to the Atlantic seaboard. Portuguese and Spanish explorers opened up great opportunities for trade in gold and spices. The flood of precious metals that flowed back into Europe over these new routes was a mixed blessing. It contributed to a steady rise in prices during the sixteenth century that created an inflation rate of about 2 % a year. The new wealth permitted research and expansion in a number of industries (printing, shipping, mining, textiles, and weapons) and led to the development of capitalist institutions and practices. There was great aggravation of the traditional social divisions.

Northern Humanist culture was largely imported from the south, but northern Humanists tended to be more socially diversified and religious. Erasmus, for example, supported a simple ethical piety in contrast to the abstract and ceremonial religion of the later Middle Ages. The best known of the early English Humanists was Thomas More (*Utopia*). In Germany, England and France, then, Humanism prepared the way for Protestant reforms and entered the service of the Catholic Church in Spain, where Jimenez de Cisneros was a key figure.

The late medieval church was a failing institution which was beset with political troubles ("Babylonian Captivity," Great Schism, conciliar movement and Renaissance papacy), and had ceased to provide an example of religious piety. Lay criticism of the church increased and became more organized.

Unlike France and England, late medieval Germany lacked the political unity to enforce national religious reforms. An unorganized opposition to Rome had formed, however, and by 1517 it was strong enough to provide a solid foundation for Martin Luther's reforms. The chapter continues with Luther's dramatic career and emphasizes his opposition to indulgences (95 Theses), his doctrine of "justification by faith alone" and his challenge to papal infallibility. In its first decade, however, the Protestant movement suffered more from internal division than from imperial interference.

Ulrich Zwingli led the Swiss Reformation on the simple guideline that whatever lacked literal support in Scripture was to be neither believed nor practiced. The unity of the Protestant movement suffered because of the theological disagreements between Zwingli and Luther and the threat of more radical groups such as the Anabaptists (who insisted upon adult baptism).

After discussing the efforts of Charles V to unify the church by formal decree (Diet of Augsburg), and the Protestant reaction and consolidation, the chapter relates the spread of Calvinism. Calvin proposed strict measures to govern Geneva's moral life which created opposition. After 1555, Geneva became a refuge for thousands of Protestants who had been driven out of France, England and Scotland. The Protestant Reformation did not take the medieval church completely by surprise. There were many efforts at internal reform before there was a Counter-Reformation. These reform initiatives did not come from the papal court, but from religious orders, especially the Jesuits. Saint Ignatius of Loyola who founded the Society of Jesus, preached self-discipline and submission to authority. The success of the Protestant Reformation led to the Council of Trent (1545-1563) which was strictly under papal control and made important reforms concerning internal church discipline; but not a single doctrinal concession was made to the Protestants.

The key precondition of the English Reformation was the "king's affair." Henry VIII wanted a papal annulment of his marriage to Catherine of Aragon. When this was refused by the pope, the "Reformation Parliament" (1529-1536) passed legislation which made the king supreme in English spiritual affairs. But despite his political break with Rome, Henry remained decidedly conservative in his religious beliefs and Catholic teaching remained prominent. During the reign of his son Edward, England fully enacted the Protestant Reformation only to have Catholicism restored by his successor, Mary. Not until the reign of Elizabeth (1558-1603) was there a lasting religious settlement achieved in England.

The next section covers the religious wars in France, Spain's attempt to win an empire, Spanish relations with England and the Thirty Years' War. Non-Lutheran Protestants were not recognized by the Peace of Augsburg. Calvinism and Catholicism were irreconcilable church systems; Calvinism was committed to changing societies and was attractive to proponents of political decentralization while Catholicism remained congenial to those who favored absolute monarchy and "one king, one church, one law." After painful experiences, some rulers known as *politiques* subordinated theological doctrine to political unity.

With few interludes, the French monarchy remained a staunch Catholic foe of the French Protestants, who were called Huguenots, until 1589. Three religious wars were fought between 1562 and 1570 and the Protestants were granted religious freedoms within their territories only to have the peace shattered by the St. Bartholomew's Day Massacre in 1572, which was supported by Catherine de Medici. Over 20,000 Huguenots were massacred on that day and Protestant reformers, who had urged strict obedience to the established political authority, now began to realize that they had to fight for their rights. Further political infighting finally resulted in the succession of the Protestant Henry of Navarre to the throne as Henry IV. Philip II of Spain was alarmed at the prospect of a Protestant France, but Henry was a *politique* and wisely converted to Catholicism while granting minority religious rights in an officially Catholic country (Edict of Nantes, 1598).

Philip II (1556-1598) inherited the western Hapsburg kingdom, where new American wealth had greatly increased Spanish power. But Spanish armies were not successful in the Netherlands, which were composed of Europe's wealthiest and most independent towns; many were also Calvinist strongholds. After 1573, the independence movement was headed by William of Orange. By 1577, a unified Netherlands forced the withdrawal of all Spanish troops. It was especially the resistance of the Netherlands that undid Spanish dreams of world empire. Although efforts to reconquer the Netherlands continued into the 1580s, Spain soon became preoccupied with England and France.

In 1585, Elizabeth I committed English soldiers to fight against the Spanish in the Netherlands. Philip launched his Armada against England in 1588, but was soundly defeated; Spain never really recovered from this defeat.

In the second half of the sixteenth century, Germany (the Holy Roman Empire) was a land of about 300 autonomous political entities (secular and ecclesiastical principalities, free cities and castle regions). Religious conflict accentuated these divisions; during this time, the population was about equally divided between Catholics and Protestants. The stage was set for the worst of the religious wars, the Thirty Years' War.

The chapter then details the conflict. About one-third of the German population died in this war which was ended by the Treaty of Westphalia in 1648. Among other provisions, it asserted the *cuius regio, eius religio* principle of the Peace of Augsburg and gave legal recognition to the Calvinists. This treaty perpetuated German division and political weakness into the modern period.

The chapter continues with a section on witchcraft and witch hunts in Early Modern Europe. An estimated 70,000 to 100,000 people were sentenced to death for harmful magic and diabolical witchcraft. Most (about 80%) of these victims were older women, spinsters or widows who were insecure, non-productive and rather vulnerable to accusation. This may have been because of a general fear by men that women were beginning to break away from their control, or that women, as midwives, were responsible for the death of children and spouses during birth. The witch hunts were the result of a general belief in the powers of magic, a belief which died with the more scientific worldview of the seventeenth century.

The Scientific Revolution is reflected in the works of the great writers and philosophers of the 17th century, who knew that they were living in a period of transition. Some embraced the new science completely, some tried to straddle the two ages, still others opposed the new developments that seemed to threaten traditional morality and had made the universe less mysterious and the Creator less loving than before. The chapter then gives brief accounts of the lives and works of Miguel de Cervantes Saavedra, William Shakespeare and John Milton.

French thought can be represented by Blaise Pascal (1623-1662), a mathematician, scientist and philosopher. Pascal believed that faith and divine grace were more necessary for human happiness than reason and science. An even more controversial religious thinker, Baruch Spinoza (1632-1677) argued that everything exists in God and cannot be conceived apart from him, a position condemned as pantheism but applauded by many late thinkers as the basis of rational religion.

The most original political philosopher of the age was Thomas Hobbes (1588-1679). An enthusiast for the new science, Hobbes advocated a commonwealth tightly ruled by law and order, free from the dangers of anarchy (*Leviathan*, 1651). A less original, but more influential political thinker was John Locke (1632-1704). Locke opposed Hobbes and denied the argument that rulers were absolute in their power; man's natural state was one of perfect freedom and equality. If a ruler failed in his responsibilities toward his subjects, he violated the social contract and could be replaced. Locke's philosophy came to be embodied in the Glorious Revolution of 1688-1689.

KEY POINTS AND VITAL CONCEPTS

1. **The Reforms of Martin Luther:** Luther focused his initial protest to Catholic doctrine on two related issues: 1) The sale of indulgences to remit temporal penalties for confessed sins and even time in purgatory was criticized by Luther, since it seemed to make salvation something that could be bought and sold 2) Indeed, salvation could be achieved, not by religious works and ceremonies, but by faith in Jesus Christ alone.

2. **The English Reformation:** The Reformation in England did not stem from religious principles as it did in Germany, but from political expediency. Henry VIII was driven by the need for a male heir, which he evidently could not obtain from his wife, Catherine of Aragon. Henry's subsequent efforts to rid himself of Catherine exemplify the subversion of religion to the political needs of state.

3. **The Spanish Armada:** As a response to growing English power and disruption of Spanish shipping and land interests, Philip II of Spain launched the Armada of 130 ships against England. The swifter English vessels together with inclement weather inflicted defeat on Spain and the loss of over one-third of her vessels. The news of the Armada's defeat gave heart to Protestant resistance. Although Spain continued to win impressive victories in the 1590s, it never fully recovered from the defeat.

4. **The Anglican Church:** One of the most skillful religious compromises attained during this period of religious war was the establishment of the Anglican Church. Elizabeth sought a compromise between Catholics and Protestants which resulted in a church which was officially Protestant in doctrine and Catholic in ritual. Extremists on either side opposed the arrangement and there were conspiracies against Elizabeth. But the compromise proved lasting (with incidental changes) to the modern day. Elizabeth was a classic *politique* and it was due to her efforts that England did not succumb to the bloody warfare on the Continent.

5. **The Renaissance and Reformation in World Perspective:** During the Renaissance, Western Europe recovered its classical heritage and established permanent centralized states and regional government. But western history between 1500 and 1650 was shaped by an unprecedented schism in Christianity. Other world civilizations maintained greater social and political unity, and remained more tolerant religiously. China managed successfully to balance the interests of the one with the many and remained more unified and patriarchal than the governments of the West. The Chinese also readily tolerated other religions (as their warm contact with Jesuit missionaries attests). There is no similar tolerance of Asian religious philosophy demonstrated by the West. Like the West, Japanese manorial society experienced a breakdown after 1467. Under Tokugawa rule (1500-1850), Japanese government stabilized and yet avoided political absolutism. Christianity was banned in the late sixteenth century as a part of an internal unification program, but Western culture would again be welcomed in the nineteenth century. The three main Islamic cultures (the Safavids in Iran, the Mughals in India, and the Ottoman empire) integrated religion with government to such an extent that they never knew the political divisiveness that dogged the West. However, the Shi'ite faction of Iran increasingly isolated itself. As in China and Japan, India too was prepared to live and learn from the West.

IDENTIFICATION TERMS

For each of the following, tell who or what it is, about when did it happen, and why it is significant in the history of the period:

indulgence (p. 457):

Huguenots (p. 469):

Jesuits (p. 468):

politiques (p. 471):

Act of Succession (p. 466):

cuius regio, eius religio (p. 465):

Charles V (p. 459):

Henry of Navarre (p. 471):

Anne Boleyn (p. 466):

Leviathan (p. 480):

Diet of Worms (p. 459):

Battle of Lepanto (p. 434):

Council of Trent (p. 469):

Edict of Nantes (p. 471):

St. Bartholomew's Day Massacre (p. 471):

MULTIPLE CHOICE QUESTIONS

1. For Europe, the late 15th and the 16th centuries were a period of
    a. unprecedented territorial expansion
    b. ideological experimentation
    c. social engineering and political planning
    d. all of the above

2. Columbus' voyage of 1492 marked the
    a. beginning of three centuries of Spanish conquest and exploitation
    b. beginning of a process that virtually destroyed the native civilizations of America
    c. rise of Spain to a major political role in Europe
    d. all of the above

3. The flood of spices and precious metals that flowed back into Europe over new trade routes
    a. contributed to a steady rise in prices during the 16th century
    b. contributed to a sudden rise in prices
    c. allowed prices to fall gradually as manufacturing was increased
    d. resulted in the institution of mercantilism

4. The most famous of the northern Humanists was
    a. Francisco Jimenez de Cisneros   c. Voltaire
    b. Desiderius Erasmus   d. Ulrich Zwingli

5. *Utopia* by Thomas More
    a. was a theological tract that supported the Catholic church
    b. depicted an imaginary society based on reason and tolerance
    c. was an expose' of human self-deception
    d. was a simple work that supported ethical piety in imitation of Christ

6. An indulgence was
    a. a payment to obtain an office in the Church
    b. a punishment meted out by the pope to heretics
    c. forgiveness given by the pope exclusively to Protestants in order to entice them back to the Church
    d. none of the above

7. Which of the following was a pamphlet written by Martin Luther?
    a. *Address to the Christian Nobility of the German Nation*
    b. *The Praise of Folly*
    c. *Institutes of the Christian Religion*
    d. *Spiritual Exercises*

8. The Diet of Worms declared that
    a. the pope's spiritual authority exceeded the temporal power of the Emperor
    b. the writings of Erasmus were to be placed on the *Index of Forbidden Books*
    c. Martin Luther was to be placed under the imperial ban and considered an outlaw
    d. both a and b

9. The Peasant Revolt of 1524 was
    a. successful in freeing the peasantry from feudal obligations
    b. supported by Martin Luther as a "Christian enterprise"
    c. condemned by Martin Luther as "unchristian" and crushed by German princes
    d. important in demonstrating that Luther was a social revolutionary

10. The reformation in Zurich was led by
    a. John Calvin   c. Philip of Hesse
    b. Ulrich Zwingli   d. Menno Simons

11. The Peace of Augsburg recognized in law what had already been established in practice:
    a. the religion of the land was determined by the Holy Roman Emperor
    b. Calvinists were to be tolerated throughout Europe
    c. Protestants everywhere must readopt old Catholic beliefs and practices
    d. the ruler of a land would determine the religion of the land

12. Calvin and his followers
    a. were motivated by a desire to transform society morally
    b. promoted a belief that only the "elect" would be saved
    c. did not depend on strict laws for governing Geneva
    d. both a and b

13. The Council of Trent (1545-1563)
    a. weakened the authority of local bishops in religious matters
    b. took steps to curtail the selling of Church offices
    c. took no steps to improve the image of parish priests
    d. changed the basic tenets of the Catholic church

14. The "King's Affair" refers to
    a. the attempt by Henry VIII to divorce Catherine of Aragon and marry Anne Boleyn
    b. Henry VIII's establishment of the Anglican church
    c. the illegitimate children fathered by Henry VIII
    d. the execution of Sir Thomas More

15. Thomas Hobbes was an important political philosopher who
    a. wrote *Treatise on Religious and Political Philosophy*
    b. argued that freedom of thought was essential to true liberty
    c. believed that people should live in a tightly controlled commonwealth
    d. both a and b

STUDY QUESTIONS

1.   What were the principal problems within the church which contributed to the Protestant Reformation? Why was the church unable to suppress dissent as it had earlier?

2.   Was the Reformation a fundamentally religious phenomenon or a generally broader development? To what extent were economic, social and cultural factors involved in the origins and spread of the Reformation? How can emphasis of the religious or non-religious character of the period alter the conception of the Reformation?

3.   What were the basic similarities and differences between the ideas of Luther and Zwingli? Luther and Calvin? Did the differences tend to split the Protestant ranks and thereby lessen the effectiveness of the movement?

4.   What was the Counter-Reformation and what principal decisions and changes were instituted by the Council of Trent? Was the Protestant Reformation a healthy movement for the Catholic Church?

5.   Why did Henry VIII finally break with the Catholic church? What "new" religion did he establish and what were its basic precepts? Did this solve the problem? What new problems did his successors face as a result of Henry's move? What was Elizabeth I's settlement and how difficult was it to impose upon all of England?

6.   Why was the Thirty Years' War fought? To what extent did politics determine the outcome of the war? Discuss the Treaty of Westphalia in 1648. Could matters have been resolved without war?

DOCUMENT QUESTIONS

1)   The Advice of a Sixteenth Century Father (p. 454):

What are the father's overriding concerns as his son leaves home for the first time? What does Christoph's father consider to be traits of a "true man"? Would Christoph's father's morality be acceptable to the church as well? Is there a religious morality in this source?

2)   German Peasants Protest Rising Feudal Exactions (p. 460):

What are the most revolutionary demands from the peasants? Do they seem reasonable given circumstances in the 16th century? Were the peasants more interested in material rather than in spiritual freedom? Was Luther right to condemn the Peasant's Revolt of 1524?

3)   *Thomas More Stands by His Conscience (p. 467):*

What were the charges levelled against Sir Thomas More by Henry VIII? Read his defense carefully. Which of his arguments do you think was most impressive?

4)   *Rules Governing Genevan Moral Behavior (p. 464):*

According to these rules, what did Calvin fear the most? Is this attempt at control inconsistent with the spiritual freedom Calvin advocated in breaking from the Catholic church? Was Geneva a theocracy with Calvin the omniscient representative of God?

MAP ANALYSIS

Map 17-2: The Empire of Charles V

Charles V became Holy Roman Emperor in 1519. He was also titled Charles I King of Spain. Study Map 17-2 on page 458 of your textbook. Note carefully the lands that were controlled by Charles. How difficult do you think it was for him to administer his possessions given the geographical fragmentation of his empire? In what ways do you think the Protestant Reformation was aided by the fact that there was no centralized political authority in the German lands that could suppress dissent?

MAP EXERCISE

Map 17-5: Religious Division About 1600

By 1600, religious allegiance was divided among four branches of Christianity. By shading in Map 17-5 provided on page 475 of your textbook and on the next page of this *Study Guide*, identify the areas dominated by the Roman Catholic Church or by one of the three largest Protestant churches, noting which church it was.

        1) Lutheran   3) Anglican

        2) Calvinist   4) Roman Catholic

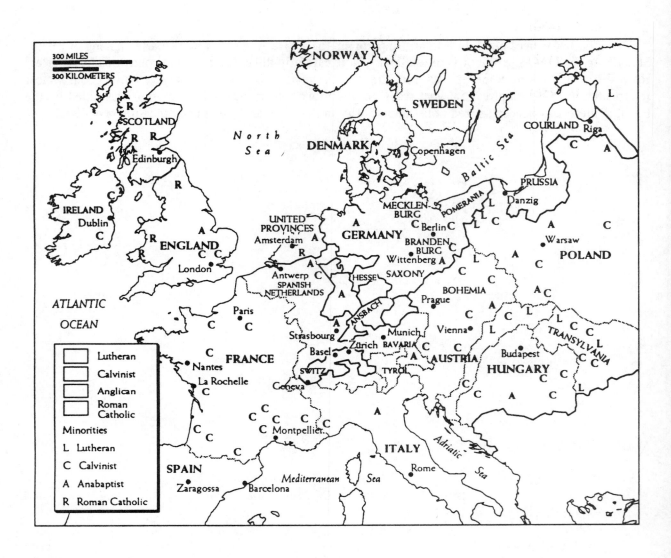

MAP 17-5
Religious Division About 1600

MULTIPLE CHOICE ANSWER KEY *(with page references)*

1. D (450)	6. D (457)	11. D (465)
2. C (450)	7. A (459)	12. D (463)
3. A (453)	8. C (459)	13. B (469)
4. B (456)	9. C (461)	14. A (466)
5. B (456)	10. B (461)	15. C (480)

18
Africa (CA. 1000-1800)

COMMENTARY

In this chapter, the authors explore, region by region, developments in Africa from 1000 to 1800. The initial focus is Africa north of the equator with its Islamic traditions, then on the coming of the Europeans. Finally, the chapter turns to East and South Africa and the effect of the Arab-Islamic and European influences in those regions.

Africa did not escape the repercussions of new developments in the Islamic and European-American worlds. The Ottoman Turks expanded into Egypt and North Africa while the Portuguese and Dutch worked the Atlantic and Indian Ocean coasts of Africa. The chapter continues by detailing Islamic activity in sub-Saharan Africa. The thriving trade in east and southeastern Africa brought Muslim merchants into the region and they extracted primary exports of ivory and slaves. From 1000 to 1500, West Africa was dominated by the Almoravids, Ghana and Mali. Mali's imperial power was built largely by the Keita King Sundiata. The greatest king proved to be Mansa Musa (r. 1312-1337). His wealth was legendary and he returned from a famous pilgrimage to Mecca in 1324 with many Muslim scholars, artists and architects. All in all, the spread of Islam was peaceful, gradual and partial. Typically, it never penetrated beyond the ruling or commercial classes of a region. Still, many innovations from architectural techniques to intellectual and administrative traditions, depended on the literate culture of Islam.

South of the Sahara, the Songhai empire was probably the strongest Muslim state in Africa and dominated the region during the fifteenth century. In 1591, the Moroccans defeated the Songhai and power shifted to the central Sudan. The state of Kanem-Bornu flourished during the seventeenth century but was reduced by famine, outside attacks and poor leadership by 1846. In the eastern Sudan, Ethiopia remained a Christian enclave, while the area between the Blue and White Niles was controlled until the mid-eighteenth century by the sultanate of the Funj.

The chapter then details events in the region of West Africa from 1500 to 1800 and emphasizes the significance of the Benin state and the importance of the Gold Coast in attracting a European presence. The Kongo kingdom of Central Africa with its Christian leader Affonso I (1506-1543) is then highlighted. Alphonso, a Christian convert, began by welcoming Jesuit missionaries and supporting conversion. But in time, he broke with the Jesuits and encouraged traditional practices, even though he himself remained a Christian. Alphonso consolidated the government, though he could not curb the more exploitative slaving practices, which contributed significantly to provincial fragmentation.

The chapter then turns to East Africa and focuses on Swahili culture and commerce. The height of Swahili civilization came during the 14th and 15th centuries. Its centers were harbor trading towns which were impressive for their fortification and stone building techniques. The trade of these coastal centers was fed by the export of inland ivory. Portuguese traders brought widespread economic desire to the east coast. Inland Africans refused to cooperate with them and the gold trade with the coast dried up. The new power center for East Africa become Zanzibar which was controlled by Omani sultans.

Finally, the authors relate the history of southern Africa and emphasize the presence of the Dutch, the organization of Cape Colony in 1652, and its transfer to British control in 1795. The slave institution set the tone for relations between the emergent and ostensibly "white" Afrikaaner population and "coloreds" of any race, free or not, all of whom could be identified with slave peoples in the colony.

KEY POINTS AND VITAL CONCEPTS

1. <u>The Spread of Islam South of the Sahara</u>: Islamic influence in sub-Saharan Africa began as early as the 8th century and by 1800 affected most of the Sudan and east coast of Africa to Zimbabwe. The process was generally peaceful, gradual, and partial. Typically, Islam never penetrated beyond the ruling or commercial classes of a region. In East Africa, Muslim traders moved down the coastline and began the "Islamization" of port towns before 800 C.E. In contrast, Islam penetrated the western and central parts of the continent by overland routes. Some major groups in West Africa strongly resisted Islamization altogether. Among them were the Mossi kingdoms founded around 1050-1170.

2. <u>The Portuguese and the Omanis of Zanzibar</u>: The decline of the original Swahili civilization in the 16th century can be attributed primarily to the waning of trade. This in turn stemmed directly from the arrival of the Portuguese and their subsequent destruction of the old oceanic trade (in particular the Islamic commercial monopoly) and of the mian Islamic city-states along the eastern coast. There was no concerted effort to spread Christianity and the religious consequences of the Portuguese presence were slight. After 1600, the Omanis shifted their home base to Zanzibar and controlled the coastal ivory and slave trades of East Africa.

3. <u>Africa (1000-1800) in World Perspective</u>: Developments in Africa history during this time varied by region. The influence of Islam reached across North Africa to the Sudan. The Islamic tradition provided a common thread of experience. At the same time, Africans from the Sahara south clung to their older traditions. On the coast, however, Islam played an important role in the development of the distinctive Swahili culture. The European voyages of discovery were especially portentous for Africa as the exploitation of the Atlantic slave trade and the Apartheid policies of the South African nation demonstrate.

IDENTIFICATION TERMS

For each of the following, tell who or what it is, about when did it happen, and why it is significant in the history of the period:

Sharif (p. 494):

Benin (p. 505):

Africaans (p. 516):

Almoravids (p. 496):

Mansa Musa (p. 500):

Sonni Ali (p. 500):

Sundiata (p. 499):

Swahili (p. 509):

Mai Dunama Dibbalemi (p. 504):

Trekboers (p. 507):

Gold Coast (p. 507):

Prazeros (p. 514):

jihad (p. 504):

"Great Zimbabwe" (p. 512):

Affonso I (p. 509):

MULTIPLE CHOICE QUESTIONS

1. By the 13th century, which of the following became the dominant religious majority in North Africa?
   - a. Sunnis
   - b. *Sharifs*
   - c. Shi'ites
   - d. Mamluks

2. After the 16th century, which political power controlled most of North Africa?
   - a. Mamluk Empire
   - b. Sharifian Empire
   - c. Ottoman Empire
   - d. Tunisian Empire

3. Muslim conversion in West and Central Africa was primarily due to the
   - a. influence of Muslim traders
   - b. breakdown of state-sponsored religion
   - c. absence of hostile Berbers from the region
   - d. Arabian fanatics

4. Which of the following was the first royal court of West Africa to convert to Islam?
   - a. Kingdom of Gao
   - b. Kingdom of Ghana
   - c. Kingdom of Mossi
   - d. Kingdom of the Moors

5. Which of the following resisted the spread of Islam into West Africa?
   - a. Fulbe
   - b. Fulami
   - c. Mossi
   - d. Kumbi

6. Which of the following developed into a notable and long-lived kingdom in the West and Central Sudan?
   - a. Ghana
   - b. Mali
   - c. Songhai
   - d. all of the above

7. In 1076, the Ghanaian state was destroyed
   - a. by Berber raiders
   - b. because of the failure of overland trade routes
   - c. by fanatical Almoravids
   - d. we cannot be certain that Ghana met its demise by 1100

8. The greatest Keita king proved to be
   - a. Sundiata
   - b. Gao
   - c. Mansa Musa
   - d. Askia Muhammad al-Turi

9. The major source of wealth for the Songhai kingdom was the
   a. coastal trade with the south
   b. ivory trade with the east
   c. caravan trade across the Sahara to the north
   d. both a and c

10. The architect of the Kanem empire in central Sudan was
    a. Sokoto   c. Maqurra
    b. Mai Dunama Dibbalemi   d. Alwa

11. A significant factor in the gradual disappearance of Christianity in the Nubian region was
    a. the apparently elite character of Christianity there
    b. the eradication of its churches by hostile tribal leaders
    c. its association with the foreign Egyptian world of Coptic Christianity
    d. both a and c

12. The lasting significance of Benin lies in its
    a. court art   c. political history
    b. government hierarchy   d. focus on human sacrifice

13. *Trekboers* were
    a. nomadic white livestock farmers in South Africa
    b. slave traders in South Africa
    c. British governmental representatives
    d. representatives of the Dutch East India Company

14. King Alfonso I of Kongo
    a. suppressed all Christianity in his kingdom
    b. halted the slave trade in his kingdom
    c. consolidated his government and remained a Christian
    d. both and c

15. The Portuguese arrival in Southeastern Africa during the first years of the 16th century
    a. led to the establishment of the Great Zimbabwe civilization
    b. was important for establishing Swahili control of the inland gold trade
    c. led to the establishment of the *Apartheid* system that was so destructive to the region
    d. was catastrophic for the East African coastal economy

1. How did Muslim control in the interior of Africa develop? Discuss the importance of trade in this area. Why did Ethiopia remain a Christian state?

2. What was the importance of the Ghana, Mali and Songhai empires to world history? Why was the control of trade across the Sahara so important to these kingdoms? What was the importance of Muslim culture to these groups? Why did all of the empires fail in these regions?

3. What was the impact of the Portuguese on the east coast of Africa? Why was this European power able to gain control of certain coastal areas in this region? What was the impact on the interior of Africa because of this development?

4. Describe the political situation of Northern Africa in the 18th century. Why did Ottoman influence decline in this region?

5. What was the "Great Zimbabwe" civilization and where did it take place? What are some of the reasons for the flowering of this civilization? What were the reasons for its demise?

6. Discuss the diversity of Cape society in South Africa. Who were the Trekboers and what was their conflict with the Khoikhoi? How was the basis for apartheid formed at this time?

DOCUMENT QUESTIONS

1)   *Ghana and Its People in the Mid-11th Century (p. 498):*

   After reading this account of Ghana by the Muslim geographer, al-Bakri, what is your impression of the civilization in Ghana? Was it well established socially and religiously? How was Ghana organized politically? What customs seem to have made the greatest impression on al-Bakri?

2)   *Muslim Reform in Songhai (p. 503):*

   What is the most important theme of this primary source? What do the questions tell you about the leadership of Muhammad al-Haghili of Songhai? What do the answers reveal about the nature of the Malidi *ulama* of which the theologian Muhammad al-Maghili was a member?

3) *Affonso I of Kongo Writes to the King of Portugal (p. 528):*

What is the topic of discussion in this letter? What are the concerns of Affonso I? Was he sincere in wanting to protect his people from European interference in the affairs of his kingdom?

4) *Visiting Mogadishu and Kilwa (p. 510):*

What Muslim values are represented in the activities and traits described in the two reports by Ibn Battuta? Does he seem to approve or disapprove of what he reports?

MAP ANALYSIS

Map 18-1: Africa Ca. 900-1500

Study Map 18-1 on page 497 of your textbook and compare it with Map 18-2 on page 501. What changes have taken place from 900 to 1800 in Africa regarding trade routes and the political control of different empires? Note in particular the inset maps of the region of West Africa.

MAP EXERCISE

Map 18-2: Africa Ca. 1500-1800

Identify the following regions, peoples, and states of Africa from about 1500-1800 on Map 18-2 on page 501 of your textbook and place them on the map provided on the next page of this *Study Guide*.

1. Ghanaian Empire

2. Asante

3. Akan

4. Songhai

5. Hausa States

6. Kongo

7. Luba

8. Lunda

9. Ndongo

10. Shona

11. Changamire

12. Cape Colony

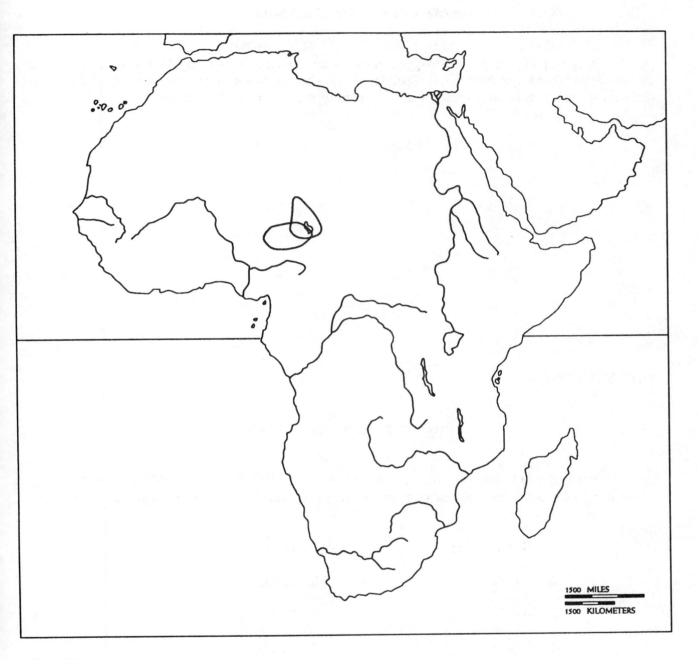

MAP 18-2
Africa ca. 1500–1800

MULTIPLE CHOICE ANSWER KEY *(with page references)*

1. A (493)	6. D (496)	11. D (504)
2. C (494)	7. D (498)	12. A (505)
3. A (495)	8. C (500)	13. A (515)
4. A (496)	9. C (501)	14. C (509)
5. C (496)	10. B (504)	15. D (512)

19

Conquest and Exploitation: The Development of the Transatlantic Economy

COMMENTARY

This chapter discusses European contacts with the Americas from voyages of discovery in the 15th and early 16th centuries to the consolidation of mercantile empires in the 17th century and the development and administration of the Atlantic slave trade.

Since the Renaissance, European contacts with the rest of the world have gone through four distinct stages: 1) discovery, exploration, initial conquest and settlement of the New World (to 1700) 2) colonial trade rivalry among Spain, France and Britain (ca. 1700-1820) 3) European imperialism in Africa and Asia (19th century) 4) decolonization of peoples previously under European rule (20th century).

The European powers administered their eighteenth century empires in accordance with the theory of mercantilism. The colonies were to provide markets and natural resources for the industries of the mother country. In turn, the latter was to furnish military security and the instruments of government. To protect its investment from competitors, each home country tried to keep a tight monopoly on trade with its colonies. The chapter then focuses on the organization and administration of the Spanish Empire, with special emphasis on the conquest of the Aztecs and the Incas.

The Spanish conquest of the West Indies, Mexico and the South American continent opened that vast region to the Roman Catholic faith. Religion, in fact, played a central role in the conquest of the New World. The mission of conversion justified military conquest and the extension of political control and dominance. As a result, the Roman Catholic Church in the New World was always a conservative force working to protect the political power and prestige of the Spanish authorities. Still, religious conversion represented an attempt to destroy a part of Native American culture, and some priests deplored the harsh conditions imposed on native peoples. The most outspoken clerical critic of the Spanish conquerors was Bartolome de Las Casas (1477-1566), a Dominican who contended that conquest was not necessary for conversion. One result of his criticism was the emergence of the "Black Legend," which characterized Spanish treatment of Native Americans as unprincipled and inhumane.

Competition for foreign markets was intense among Britain, France and Spain. In North America, their colonists quarreled endlessly over the territory, fishing rights, fur trade and relationships with the Indians. Above all, they clashed over the West Indies, the lucrative producers of coffee, tobacco and especially sugar - and ready purchasers of African slaves. The chapter then focuses on the nature of slavery in the Americas, the plantation economy and the transatlantic slave trade that linked Europe, Africa, and the European colonies in South America, the Caribbean, and North America. Recent scholarship estimates that at a minimum Africa lost some thirteen million people to the Atlantic trade alone in addition to another five million exported to the oriental trade. The African slaves who were transported to the Americas were converted to Christianity. They became largely separated from African religious outlooks, though some African practices survived in muted forms. This conversion represented another example of the crushing of a set of non-European cultural values in the context of the New World economies and social structures.

European settlers in the Americas were generally prejudiced against black Africans, thinking them to be savage or less than civilized. Although racial thinking in regard to slavery became more important in the 19th century, the fact that slaves were differentiated from the rest of the population by race, as well as by their status as chattel property, was fundamental to the system.

The chapter then goes on to discuss the history and process of slaving in Africa, as well as the oriental and occidental slave trade. Between 1640 and 1690, the number of slaves sold to European traders doubled, increasing the growing participation of Africans in the expanding trade. These developments accelerated in the 18th century as the demands of expanding plantation economies fueled the trade. However, as European and American nations began to outlaw slaving in the early 19th century, occidental demand slowed and prices sank. Although the oriental trade continued, indigenous African slavery began a real decline only at the end of the 19th century in part because of the dominance of European colonial regimes and in part because of internal changes.

KEY POINTS AND VITAL CONCEPTS

1. Mercantilism: The early modern European empires of the 16th through 18th centuries existed primarily to enrich trade. To the extent that any formal theory lay behind the conduct of these empires, it was mercantilism. Economic writers of the time believed that a nation had to gain a favorable balance of gold and silver bullion. Colonies existed to provide markets and natural resources for the industries of the home countries. In turn, the home country furnished military security and political administration. The home country and its colonies were to trade exclusively with each other through a restrictive and complex system of tariffs and navigation laws. National monopoly was the ruling principle. Mercantilist ideas often did not mesh with the economic realities of the colonies. Colonial demands for relative economic independence often clashed with the welfare of the mother country and were met with even greater restrictions and punitive action. For all these reasons, the 18th century became the "golden age of smugglers."

2. The African Slave Trade: Slavery is one of the oldest of human institutions and virtually every premodern state in history depended on it to some extent. The African slave trade must be seen as part of the larger commercial system of Atlantic trade between Europe, Africa and European colonies in North and South America and the Caribbean. The system was directed to exploitation of the New World and thus the slave trade grew not from racist principles (although they were used as justification), but from colonial economic needs. The major sources for slaves were the Kongo-Angola region and the Guinea coast. Well over twelve million persons were lost to Africa through the Atlantic trade. Taken as a whole, the slave trade varied in extent quite sharply from period to period with its peak in the eighteenth century and its demise in the nineteenth. The effects of the slave trade on Africa are not easy to assess. It appears that slavery was a result, not a cause of regional instability and change; increased warfare meant increased prisoners to be enslaved and sold off. Finally, the slave trade produced Africa's major diaspora, which was also one of the major migrations of global history. From an American perspective, it was an important element in the formation of our modern society.

3. Early Spanish Conquests: The conquests of Mexico and Peru stand among the most dramatic and brutal stories in modern world history. One civilization armed with advanced weapons subdued, in a remarkably brief time, two powerful peoples. But beyond the bloodshed, these conquests marked a fundamental turning point of world civilizations. Never again in the Americas would native American peoples and their values have any significant impact or influence.

4. The Transatlantic Economy in World Perspective: The contact between the native peoples of the American continents and the European explorers of the 15th and 16th centuries transformed world history. America's native peoples encountered Europeans intent on conquest, exploitation and religious conversion. Because of their technological superiority in weaponry and the impact of disease, Europeans were able to achieve a rapid conquest. In both North and South America, economies of exploitation were established that relied on native labor to feed extensive plantation systems. Slaves were imported from Africa drawing Europeans, Africans, and Americans together in a vast world wide web of production based on slave labor. The Atlantic slave trade's impact on the history of the Americas and of the United States in particular continues to be felt in the development of laws and societal concerns such as racism.

IDENTIFICATION TERMS

For each of the following, tell who or what it is, about when did it happen, and why it is significant in the history of the period:

corregidores (p. 526):

James Oglethorpe (p. 531):

Treaty of Tordesillas (p. 527):

mercantilism (p. 520):

Hernan Cortes (p. 521):

repartimiento (p. 525):

Black Legend (p. 523):

encomienda (p. 524):

conquistadores (p. 523):

quinto (p. 523):

Bartolome de Las Casas (p. 523):

Jamestown (p. 533):

Casa de Contratacion (p. 527):

peninsulares (p. 525):

hacienda (p. 525):

MULTIPLE CHOICE QUESTIONS

1. What was chiefly responsible for European dominance over so much of the world from the 16th-19th centuries?
   a. innate cultural superiority
   b. technological advantage
   c. increased emphasis on learning and universities
   d. advantageous diplomacy

2. In the New World, *audiencias* were
   a. judicial councils   c. jails for smugglers
   b. governors   d. religious audiences

3. In the New World, *conquistadores* were
   a. foot soldiers   c. local officers
   b. municipal councils   d. judicial councils

4. *Creoles* were
   a. people of mixed racial composition
   b. those born in the New World whose ancestry was European
   c. slaves from Central America who were sold in Caribbean ports
   d. those whose status improved due to reforms by Charles III

5. The African slave trade
   a. was rather narrow in its scope, directed as it was toward European markets
   b. must be seen as a part of a larger commercial system
   c. was directed to the exploitation of the New World
   d. both b and c

6. James Oglethorpe founded Georgia as a
   a. commercial colony which would produce tobacco for the English crown
   b. refuge for English debtors
   c. haven for Protestant religious liberty
   d. haven for the Catholic minority in the colonies

7. The *encomienda* was a
   a. land grant
   b. formal grant by the crown to the labor of a specific number of Native Americans for a particular time
   c. complicated system of bullion trade
   d. trading contract

8. The Spanish crown
    a. advocated the *encomienda* system
    b. voluntarily destroyed the *encomienda* system in the 17th century
    c. disliked the *encomienda* system because it created a powerful independent nobility
       in the New World
    d. both b and c

9. The Spanish monarchy received approval from Catholic church authorities for a policy of military
   conquest in Latin America
    a. only with strict guidelines against exploiting the native population
    b. upon signing the Treaty of Torsedillas
    c. on the grounds that conversion to Christianity justified actions of the state
    d. both a and b

10. Religious conversion of Native Americans by the Catholic Church
    a. brought acceptance of European culture
    b. resulted in a very large percentage of Native Americans in the priesthood
    c. represented an attempt to destroy another part of Native American culture
    d. both a and b

11. By far the most effective and outspoken clerical critic of the Spanish conquistadors was
    a. Bartolome de las Casas   c. Jimenez de Cisneros
    b. Junipero Serra   d. none of the above

12. One of the most important forces that led to the spread of slavery in Brazil and the West Indies was
    the
    a. cultivation of tobacco   c. *encomienda* system
    b. cultivation of sugar   d. presence of small landowners in these areas

13. African slaves who were transported to the Americas
    a. generally converted to various Christian religious sects
    b. converted only to Protestantism
    c. maintained their African religions
    d. rejected their old religions and accepted the nature gods of the New World

14. The institution of slavery persisted in the Americas until the
    a. 18th century   c. 19th century
    b. 20th century   d. 17th century

15. In Brazil, the economy was
    a. more dependent on Indian labor than in Spanish America
    b. less dependent on Indian labor than in Spanish America
    c. stable without slavery
    d. strictly regulated by the government

STUDY QUESTIONS

1. How did the Spanish organize their empire in the Americas? Was this an efficient operation economically?

2. What role did the Catholic Church play in the pacification of Native American civilizations?

3. Describe the *encomienda* system. How did it differ from the *repartimiento*? Why was the *hacienda* such a dominant institution in rural and agricultural life?

4. Describe the Atlantic slave trade. Where were slaves obtained and how were they treated? How did slavery affect the economy of the transatlantic trade?

5. Discuss mercantilism in theory and practice. What were its main ideas? Did they work? Which European country was most successful in establishing a mercantilist empire? Why?

6. What were the main reasons for colonial conflict between Britain, Spain, and France in the Americas? How did the triangles of trade function between the Americas, Europe, and Africa?

DOCUMENT QUESTIONS

1) *The Portobello Fair (p. 530):*

What was the Portobello Fair and why was it important? What kinds of goods were traded there according to this primary source? What general statements about Spanish control of trade in the western hemisphere can you make after reading this document?

2) *A Contemporary Describes Forced Indian Labor at Potosi (p. 526):*

After reading this primary source, what examples of brutality on the part of the Spanish toward the Indians of the area stand out in your mind? How would you compare the treatment of Native Americans as noted in this passage with that of African slaves en route to America (see p. 540)? Was there any difference between the "forced labor" of Indians and the slavery of Black slaves?

3)   *A Slave Trader Describes the Atlantic Passage (p. 540):*

According to the journal of Thomas Phillips, why was the passage from Africa across the Atlantic so dangerous? Why did slave ships continue to make these transport voyages if passage was so dangerous?

4)   *The Slave Ship (p. 539):*

Analyze the diagram of the slave ship *Brookes* on page 539 of your textbook. What can you tell about the nature of the Atlantic slave trade from this loading plan? Compare this with the written account of the Atlantic passage by Thomas Phillips on page 540. What is the general view of black Africans that emerges from this comparison?

MAP ANALYSIS

Map 19-1: Viceroyalties in Latin America in 1780

Analyze Map 19-1 on page 528 of your textbook. What is a viceroyalty and how did Spain effectively rule its land claims in the Americas? Do you think Spain was overextended? What competitors did it face? Explain why such organization was necessary, according to mercantilist theories?

MULTIPLE CHOICE ANSWER KEY *(with page references)*

1. B (522)	6. B (531)	11. A (523)
2. A (536)	7. B (524)	12. B (527)
3. A (533)	8. C (524)	13. A (534)
4. B (525)	9. C (523)	14. C (536)
5. D (533)	10. C (523)	15. B (527)